Onward, Dad Words

Garrison Somers

Blotter Books

Text copyright 2025 by Garrison Somers

First Printing 2025
All rights reserved. No part of this publication may be
reproduced, or transmitted in any form or by any means,
electronic or mechanical, including photocopying, recording or any
information storage and retrieval system, without the written permission
of the author.
Somers, Garrison 1957 -
Onward, Dad Words
ISBN 979-8-985-9878-8-1

Published in the United States by Blotter Books
an imprint of The Blotter Magazine, Inc.
1010 Hale Street, Durham, NC 27705
Cover and author photos used with permission.
Printed and bound in the USA

Onward, Dad Words

by Garrison Somers

To the women - my wife, my daughters,
my mother and mother-in-law, my sisters -
each and all of whom made me
the best of what I am.

Doldrums – November 2016-January 2017

Part 1 – *Quite some number of summers ago, I was a sailor.*

OK, that's not completely true - I was actually the totally subservient, no decision making at all, weak-skilled side-kick to a sailor. The crew. Being 'crew' was sloggingly hard work, mostly involving waking up at the spur of the weather-decision-making moment on Saturday mornings at a remarkably Godawful hour to ride in my friend's family station wagon to the "yacht club" to pick up the trailer with our boat on it, tow it to the "yacht club" where we were going to be sailing that day, then putting the boat in the water and leading, or more often following, other sailors in boats around courses for a couple of hours in the summer sun or rain until we could go home again.

There. That's what happened, most June and July weekends throughout the 1980s. Sounds like good work if you can get it, right? And if I left the story just like that, you might wonder what was wrong with me in my youth, that I didn't just enjoy the ride. Piss-poor storytelling on my part.

So let me try and start again.

As I remember it, I always loved the inexorable arrival of summer sailing. I appreciated everything that led up to it, all of the preparation and fiddling around. I didn't sail when I was growing up, because the closest thing to a body of water we had near us was the Passaic River. Maybe if there had been a lake nearby? Maybe if we'd been near the ocean? I don't know. (The best thing I can say about the Passaic was that it flooded from time to time. The worst is that for a while it was one of the most polluted rivers on planet Earth. By the way, you don't win trophies for that.) So when I grew up, it became a big deal to live near the ocean, an even bigger deal to have the opportunity to be able to join a sailing club. I was Ishmael, coming from the land, intending to go to sea. Without a lick of sailing experience. Ready to drown at the hand of mother nature. And what I lacked in legacy, cool clothes and any sailing chops whatsoever, I more than made up in unbridled willingness. Is that a thing?

While the soot-gray snow still rested in waist-high piles around the parking lot at work, I would begin to get the sailing itch. Between incoming tech-support calls, I did my "dips" – slowly raising and lowering myself in my chair with only my arms, over and over again. I tried to be surreptitious about it, but my call-center co-workers stared. *What are you doing?* the more curious might ask. *Oh, I'm pumping water out of my boat, of course.* Sit-ups on the floor at home while watching *The A-Team* or *Moonlighting* to strengthen my flabby winter belly so I could hike-out for long reaches, my feet through stirrups on the deck and my backside hanging dangerously over the transom, my weight counterbalancing us against the push of the wind.

April. I was squatting on a stack of old kapok lifejackets in my friend's garage while he tinkered with the sailboat. All winter out of the water, the craft was as leaky as...as any wooden thing originally designed to float on water but which was so old and so full of tiny holes in the seams between hull planks that who now could tell if it would ride above or beneath the surface more effectively. My friend had a pre-springtime ritual of endlessly talking about caulk options and strange splines and waterproofing products with cool names like Marine Tex, and sometime during Lent and making the Big Decision come Palm Sunday. He would then wisely use the school Spring Break week (either before or after Easter, depending) to carefully hand-scrape the hull of the boat and slather on the new stuff, which we consistently called "Go-Fast" no matter who made it, what was promised, and how well it worked. If it kept the water out, it was deferential entitlement. If the marine lacquer failed us, leaving me pumping out water with my mighty office-chair-dip arms somewhere out on the bay in mid-July, well, it was scathing sarcasm. Note: the Go-Fast never seemed to permit an outer paint job, so our boat - *Gizmo*, she was called - was butt-ugly, even among other ancient wooden sailboats of the same design.

The sail was un-bagged to cursorily check for wear and tear. It was worn and near-torn, and if I'm not mistaken, as old as the boat itself. It had a deep belly, which I was instructed made it better for heavier air, or what normal people call windy days. The sail's wood battens were inspected for cracks, bends and breaks. We looked at stays, centerboard, rudder, tiller, mast, boom, and all of the other tools-of-the-sailing-trade, to determine whether they had weathered winter as well as could be expected. Nothing was ever replaced with new. I don't actually know why. Maybe, like us, the bits and parts were supposed to get one year older and still go out on the Bay on summer Saturdays. If there were new cracks, we bound them, ironically enough, with white medical tape.

In May I got my yard mowed, the gardening done. Spring Saturdays were for puttering around, but also for acclimating my pale Anglo skin to summer's upcoming *beneficial rays* of the sun. I checked to be sure I had a supply of zinc-oxide for my nose, cheeks and the tops of my ears. New sunscreen for my arms, neck, tops of my legs. I wouldn't cut the grass again until August, having no free Saturdays to do so. By then it would bolt to seed and the lovely but untamable Rose-Of-Sharon bush growing in the front yard would spread its wiry rhizomes across my yard and into the neighbor's. Ah, well. (I find it strange that in that place and time, RoS was a garden pest, while here it is a wonder.)

A typical early-May conversation with myself: Hey, something died in my sailing kitbag. Holy crap! Not my boat-shoes! Why didn't I wash them and put them out to dry the last time I wore them? When was that? Oh, that can't be good. Take a pail of water and some Dawn dish detergent a scrub brush and begin carefully cleaning them. See, the salt comes out of the leather - Sperry Topsiders are able to withstand a fair amount of abuse. But some of the stitching in one sole is starting to fray. You'll need a new pair soon - may as well go this weekend.

But my willingness, my enthusiasm for being out there on the water, for *sailing*, would only get me so far. I was to be "crew" forever. I had missed out on that other nautical growing-up education curriculum, what with my center-of-the-state, riding my bicycle past the blackberry brambles, bobbing up and down in the lukewarm water of the community pool, playing whiffle-ball all evening growing-up summers. No beach, no lake, not even a cow-pond. My friend, the skipper of our boat, was a child of the shore; with three decades of learning watery nuance of each "yacht" club's course, and the mysterious proclivities of the wind. I was a forever-novice, would never accumulate the experience to sail against my friend and the other sailors in our class of boat. Not to mention that there were but sixteen of these boats, each between thirty and fifty years old. Perhaps, I dreamed, I could have one made by one of the old builders? Ha. I would need to win the lottery. Or sell my house. (And each November I could sneak into the other fellows' garages and poke holes in their hulls with an ice-pick, just to even the odds…)

No, I had to reluctantly accept if not embrace that I was along as ballast. Admit to myself it was sufficient that my friend woke in the pre-dawn hours of a summer Saturday morning and stuck his head out the front door for a weather-check. If it was windy, or raining, or windy and raining, he called on me to add weight.

On ring one I shook myself awake (literally - it was, I am sure, a weird thing to see), found my lanolin-smelly Peter Storm sweater and waited silently on the front porch for him to drive up the road. Closed my eyes in the passenger seat, woke when we got to McDonald's (two egg mcmuffins and two orange juices) ate like it was my last meal ever and immediately nodded off again. Note: Down-bay racing was perfect for a power nap, up-bay not so much.

To my constant chagrin, other sailors actually looked like sailors. Their eyes were crinkled at the corners from being out in the sun so much. Their own spring-refreshed tans more...tan. I don't know why, but perhaps a childhood filled with *community pool* sunshine doesn't compare to Bay sun. Those fellows with zinc-oxide slathered on their noses (although it was but seven in the blessed AM. And overcast. With a good chance of rain) looked more like *warriors in war-paint*, while I just looked like a nerd. Or rather, more nerdish than usual. Their sweaters seemed more casually ragged than mine, and they wore ballcaps that didn't have logos on them, just sweat-salt lines and an elegant fading of the original colors into something not named on the Pantone palette. I wore shorts, a tee-shirt, my sweater tied around my waist, my hair cut for the weekday workplace. My face was, well, mine. I was, I knew because I'd been told, a *bennie*: someone only recently here, temporary, merely enjoying the beneficial rays. You could probably look it up. Bennie, noun, a term of derision with regards to sailing. Someone likely to leave before the end, to give up under the strain. Out of place, no matter how much they participate. Gomer Pyle was probably a gunnery sergeant when he left the Marine Corps to move back home to Mayberry, but he was still Gomer Pyle.

Or maybe my hands gave me away, never certain where to place them as we arrived. Carrying the sailbag under one arm, our McDonald's breakfast trash in the other hand, looking for a can to dump it in. I was always self-conscious.

My friend and I readied our boat. I worked very hard at looking like I knew what I was doing. Or at least trying to look like I knew what my friend wanted me to do. Competent. Pushing the heavy things. Towing the heavy things. Lifting the heavy things. Barge, bale, etc. Burned all of the breakfast calories in one fell swoop. And then waiting in the rain like a wet cat at the front door, while my friend the skipper signed our boat in. If it was raining, I got wet and stayed wet. If it was raining, well, I got cold. If it was raining and windy, I got cold and scared.

Part 2 – God, your sea is so large and my boat so small.

So then, what was there to be scared about? I could swim and the water wasn't particularly deep, wasn't very cold by June and less so in July. Still my heart thumped uncomfortably in my chest with something other than excited anticipation.

Our boat rigged, we pushed away from the dock in our turn and pointed ourselves down-river. I always clambered aboard first; all clutching hands and clumsy feet, to get to my spot as carefully as possible. Although the boat was fifteen feet long, it drew but five inches of water. That is it only settled five inches into the water when empty. And the boat's hull was curved and the centerboard was up when we lowered the boat into the river with the mechanical lift – a kind of boat-crane - so there was little to prevent it from tipping and spilling me out as I unhooked the lift's cables. I, on the other hand, was that counterbalancing thing - that ballast - when my friend climbed aboard. He had a sense about him of being at ease on this wobbly paper cup floating on the river. He stood on the bow, hoisted the gaff and sail, tied off those lines, and seemed to stroll thoughtlessly back to his place at the tiller.

With 150 square feet of sail, Gizmo was a touchy creature. A gust of breeze at the wrong time could tip her. That is, a bit of wind and an unready, unsteady (me, in a nutshell) crewmember. A tip and the race was over, particularly because the boat we chose to sail seemed to be designed to take in water quickly and go down with all hands. Not that you could honorably drown like a normal sailor. Instead, you had to float in the Bay beside your overturned boat until the committee boat arrived to look down at you with hands on hips and scornful smirks. And what happened here? they wouldn't ask, didn't have to. Now you had to un-step the mast, tie it all up with the sail to the boat as best as you could so that you could be towed ignominiously to the closest dock. *No,* one might decide in that situation, *please don't bother. Just load the starter gun with real slugs and put us out of our misery!*

While I made sure that everything was stowed - our lifejackets, the hand-pump, we slid before the morning breeze down river to the course with its beach-ball shaped marker "barrels" moored in place against in the river's mouth to the Bay. The rain, which might have postponed the race until the afternoon, or indeed some other Saturday, was slacking. The wind remained stiff, however. Good, I told myself. I'm here, we're ready. Let's race! But the truth was I always felt like a novice, like a liar, because I couldn't get my heart to settle down, couldn't *stow* my anxiety, relax and have fun. All I wanted to do, once I was out on the water, was be done. How long until we get to start? How long was the race itself? Now that the rain was gone there was little likelihood of a "scratch," so we'd do our race. Uh-oh. Would they have two races, perhaps, this morning, instead of one in the morning and one after lunch? That would be good. How nice it would be to be done for the day when lunchtime came.

We were in a cluster of other racers of different sail-shapes and hull styles, tacking forth and back in the fresh Bay breeze (read gusty wind, with unpredictable changes in direction) determining the best positioning for us prior to the start of our race. A beautiful collection of different colored sails, like birds on the wing. We watched the other classes, my friend nodding as one by one they were off with a blast of the committee boat's air-horn. He already knew what to do but was looking left and right to see what the other sailors in our class were doing. *What are they thinking?* his squinting eyes asked. The first leg looked to be a broad reach - wind coming at a 90-degree angle to the boat. A straight shot to the "barrel," it would be like runners racing to the first curve in the cinder track. *Great fun, all of the boats being tested against one another. Pinch at the barrel, and take a big curve without jibing to conserve speed. Go out to clear air as long as possible, then come about and make a run back at the second barrel. Yes.* Strategic knowledge I didn't have (like not completely understanding wind direction versus *apparent* wind direction), and was not able to just...access, despite this not being my first rodeo. Or even my second.

And so my constant thought was *would that this were already over!*

And that, ladies and gentlemen, was the story of my life. I was terrible at just being in the moment, and doing what that moment required. I was terrific at preparing - oh, my arms were now as strong as steel cable. OK, maybe copper cable. And I was good at being done, great at cleaning up and leaving quietly. But I didn't have much stomach for being in the here, and now.

Not just because the weather sucked (or, rather, blew.) Or because I didn't fit in with the salty bastards who sailed every summer Saturday. I kind of understood all of that. It was a club, after all, and they let me be here, as crew. As ballast. But I was also like this at work, at home. Back in school? Good at studying, lousy at being in the classroom. In the office, I was good at preparing for the sale, not happy speaking in front of the customer. Just super at driving home after the dinner date was over.

The fourth firing of the starter's pistol still made my heart jump a beat. We timed our getaway to perfection out of the chaos of other boats, and I was leaning back as my friend pulled the sheet that controlled the sail just a bit tighter. My feet tucked beneath the straps, my legs and belly burned with the effort of keeping us upright against the wind. I wished I had a drink of water and was simultaneously glad I didn't have to pee. Go figure.

And that, I thought, must be the thing. I'm from *land*. I don't know how many years of being out here every Saturday it takes to be comfortable out here. (God! I hurt already. My hands ached from helping set the mast, from holding on to the transom, from white-knuckled gripping in anticipation. My stomach muscles ached from being someone trapped in an office chair every Monday through Friday.) Maybe it's an undefinable number. I would never get there, would never fit in, would never get to the point where I'm not frightened. Stop thinking, I told myself. Inhale, smell the salt and the Bay and the exhaust from motor boats and the pong of mildewed lifejackets. Exhale and sail.

Part 3 – There is nothing exciting about watching a sailing race.

Unless you are a sailor, or some commentator is yammering in your ear about the trigonometry of speed and distance, it is almost impossible to see who is winning or in a better position to win from the cluster of things moving back and forth across the water. When we watch the lovely classic film *Captains Courageous*, who can figure out what Lionel Barrymore is thinking when he is so far behind the fishing boat he's trying to beat to market. Cut across what? Why doesn't Freddy Bartholomew ask the question for us? What *are* shoals and why not go through them? And anyone watching on this Saturday would have wondered why we even bothered. We were slow. Our class of sailboats for all their sail, were always slow. We looked as if one might swim faster between barrels. Hell, *walk* faster.

But when you are out there, it is all about the wind. Wind is not invisible at all. It is blowing in your face, your ears, on the back of your neck - kicking salt-flavored, river-musked spray up off the bow. Pointing the dangling tell-tales in a peculiar direction, rippling the sun-dappled water in a place off in the distance. It is there behind you, blocked by another crew's 150 square feet of sail with a different number on it. It is following other sails whose crews fight to control them, or not following other sails whose crews struggle with slackened sheets, trying to find an elusive puff. As much as being a game with other sailors, sailing is a game with a life-force called wind.

It is also the pain in your shins and your back and arms. It is the heady risk of taking a second to grab the hand-pump to bail out some of the water sloshing over my Topsiders. Water weighs eight pounds per gallon. I'll bet you didn't know that. Get a gallon out of the boat, two, and it's a few inches per hundred yards of speed. In a mile, that's the length of a boat. It is thoughtful and exciting, yes. It is also fearful.

Everything seemed to me to be about to go wrong. I scootched down in the boat to grab the pump. Tugged-and-shoved the plastic handle like a madman, like a dervish doing a breakdance, to get as much water out as possible. *Hike out!* my friend shouted. I instantly dropped the pump, leaning like I might dip the back of my head in the Bay, get completely soaked. That's why I was here, I thought. I'm heavy. Well, thank God I'm heavy! Where did that blast of wind come from? It shoved us ahead a couple knots faster, but it almost took us over. Did anyone else get it? Did they tip? No time to look around. One second of looking around like that and everything can go wrong. The wind shifts and there's an uncontrolled jibe - the sail catches wind and the heavy boom is now coming at the back of your head, or worse, missing the back of your head and swinging out wildly to pull the whole boat over. And you can't look everywhere at once. You cannot actually predict what might happen next. It's nothing at all like driving, or walking down a street or leaning back on a couch and watching sailing. It's *sailing*.

Past the first barrel. Everyone else had already come about - turned and pointed themselves at the second barrel. We were counting on the Bay being at full-high-tide with no current against us. *Ready to come about!* my friend finally shouted his warning. *Come about!* He knew that I didn't need to respond, didn't even have the breath to. We moved to the other side as swiftly and carefully as two full-grown men can on a little wooden boat. The boom - so aptly named - swung past my head, the lines sweeping my hair. *We're on another long reach now, while they're tacking,* my friend shouted - information that sort of made sense to me. Our opponents would have to change direction a few times, slowing each time they did so, while we could just keep on going in this direction at this speed for most of the leg. Yes, indeed, as long as the wind held. And if there was a brief opportunity to bail some of the water – eight pounds of weight per gallon – out of Gizmo's hull. And if the sail did what it was supposed to do and we could lean back and hold her steady and true. Strategy!

But this story is not a sailing lesson. You've probably had quite enough of nautical terms, and you're not on the water yourself (as I said earlier, sailing!) You don't care about the labor pains, you just want to see the baby.

We were so far away from everyone else that we could see it unfold. The clouds that had held the rain (and the wind, it turned out) were dissipating, drifting over the distant highway 35 bridge. The July sun was out, it was warm (suddenly) and we hit a patch of dead air (a place with breeze at all.) Our forward motion slowed and we watched the other boats take the turn and head for the finish line. Come about, my friend said, seeing a puff (wind rustling the water, out there somewhere off to port.) We did, and halfway through the movement our sail was luffing – just sitting there - and the boom wouldn't go over any farther and so we used the paddle to push it out to try and force ourselves on. And sat there. And sat there some more.

The breeze did pick up a little, eventually. We went around the barrel and poked slowly to the finish line. By the time we crossed, in last place, the Bay was beginning to turn to glass, in that way it occasionally would, my skipper said. He was smoking a cigarette and I was using the pump to get the last water out of Gizmo's hull. The committee kept looking around and checking weather reports on the radio and such, to determine if there was going to be enough wind at all, perhaps after lunch, to have the second race. With a bullhorn they announced that it was a wait-and-see. All of the sailboats crept back up the river to the club. Most had to paddle the last hundred yards or so, ignominiously, sheepishly. Along the shoreline beauties bathed, Huckleberries swung out over the water on rope swings, and for all we knew juleps were sipped.

Waiting ashore for the committee boat's final decision, my friend fetched our box-lunches, provided by the host club. I sat in wet shorts, shirt and sweater, gnawed through my ham and swiss sub like a convict escaped from Devil's Island. My God, yes! - Fritos Corn Chips! Dr. Pepper! What had I done to deserve such riches? Full, I became sleepy again, and in the back of my mind, I wanted our day to be done. What could top this - to be tired and wind-burned and only slightly soggy and in last place? Let the sea-breezes go, Neptune. We were done with it. I sat by a tree and closed my eyes. An hour later, my friend woke me to tell me sadly that the second race was cancelled. I tried to look suitably discouraged, but my energy in getting Gizmo out of the water and back on her trailer gave me away, I'm sure.

And if they had decided on a second race after lunch, I wouldn't have gone anyway - remember, I was only ballast for windy days. I would have sat on the club lawn, looking down the river, like a dog whose master has gone to work. Club members showing up might have wondered who I was, why I was on their property. *Is that a sailor, or just some...homeless guy? Go ask. No, you go ask.* Staying ashore might have been worse than going back out. I don't know.

In any case, we hooked the trailer up to the family wagon, and pointed ourselves due north, heading back to our club to put Gizmo away. Did you have a good time? my friend asked. Yes, I replied. I did. At that moment, it was not a lie.

Road Trip – May 2017

Duke Hospital is beautiful. I went there, recently, to have an MRI because I was told to. I'm not a fan of MRI's, nor going to hospitals, but with all of the current political malaise I know better than to complain that I have people watching out for my health, so I did what I was told to. Also, I was promised sedation, so there's that. I woke up at dawn's crack because I insisted on showering. I was always instructed to be as clean as possible when doctors are going to probe you. You know, so they won't talk about you during coffee breaks. Do doctors actually take coffee breaks? I never see it on TV. Sex, yes. Coffee? Hmm. Maybe. But not so much chit-chat about hygiene of patients.

Anyway, we were off before rush-hour traffic. The girls were left to their own devices, making their lunches, waiting for the ride to school. Elder had been nervous for a few days – what is wrong with Dad? Younger, not so much. I think she's pretty sure she has a bead on things, what kinds of things happen in her world and which don't. Water-main break so we can't take showers for a day or so? Yes. Dad really sick? Nope. I like her thinking, although it has no basis in science or logic.

Drive, park, walk - moving about in that herky-jerky modern civilization way we do. A significant part of my life. More than I would choose – I'm not much of a traveler or a tourist. I prefer to sit and read, or take a walk outside and come home and sit and read.

I followed herself into the facility - it was a cool morning, almost crisp and the sun's glare was welcome. I was beginning to feel that fight or flight thing I am reliably told is an instinct, but which I also think is ingrained habit. I seem to need to be more than just cajoled to do things outside my comfort zone, which extends all the way out to the sidewalk in front of the house and out back only to the patch of ground I'm turning into a rose garden. My brain wants to find reasons not to go out on the town. This is defined as social anxiety, folks. So this morning I kept pushing one foot in front of the other, across the street, along with the nurses, doctors, students, other patients, administrators, attendants, visitors, vendors…

Into the enormous hospital building. Correction – hospital *complex*. My vision, in such situations, gets pretty, well, tunnely. Where do I need to be, what do I do when I get there, how soon until I can leave? I did look from side to side, occasionally, because I didn't want to bump into people who wanted to arrive at their appointments somewhere faster than I did. There was a big entrance hall, like a hub of a wheel with hallways for spokes.

We chose a spoke. One wall was windows, open to green space; draped with that kind of ivy and tree which does well enough in the areas shaded by tall buildings. The other wall had paintings on it, Impressionistic prints, I guessed. Pretty. Reaching the end of the hall, we turned left and saw that we had run out of hall without achieving our goal. Oops. Herself hung another left into a waiting room – not ours - and stood in line to ask the woman at the desk where we should be. In a minute, the woman corrected our directions. Off we toddled.

Outside again, we saw the next building, our building, had our *ah-ha* moment, and made our way through the fractal flow of people and into the coffee shop. I said nothing. *No coffee for you*, I told myself. I actually had the presence of mind to imagine I had a yearning for coffee that took precedence over my fear of that which was coming in my morning. Maybe some coffee later? Again, a positive sign, that I could imagine a later, after what was coming. *Good*, I told myself. *Good boy*.

So we signed in. And then someone came to get me. I mean, someone like a concierge. *My person*. Fast, as in expeditiously enough that I didn't really have time to boot up my fight or flight simulation software. (Would I ever just get up and leave? Probably. Even if my wife was there, and didn't chase after me and had to catch a cab home? I really don't know, and don't want to know.)

My person talked, about what was going to happen next. Did I know? No? OK, then, here's the deal. He spoke softly, almost conspiratorially, as if how I should take off all my clothes and put on two robes – one backwards and one...frontwards so I was comfortably covered up was a secret he didn't reveal to every patient. How to secure everything in a locker, even though herself was right there. It was, not surprisingly, effectively reassuring. It would be easy, he said. He would be there with me the whole time. And he nearly literally handheld me through the discussion about medication and how it was going to make the next hour so much better. So much.

I won't explain the details – I know we've all been through something similar to it. It is difficult to describe personal fears. Fine authors make a decent living doing it. Suffice to say that finished, still floating somewhat, I dressed to go home.

Herself led our way back along the hallways. Someone was playing a grand piano downstairs in an atrium. An employee, she explained. Further along, a small fireplace burned behind glass, the heat from it going somewhere else as the day was now warm and the hallway comfortable. People were sitting nearby, looking at the flames for portents or the calming relief or the magic held within their flicker.

Around the corner, a young woman in scrubs was playing a violin. On her break. A bit further, two women were talking, one in tears, the other – in scrubs – hugging her.

Down the long hallway, with paintings proudly hung along one wall, with lights and little cards for title and artist. I stopped to look. I was in no hurry, not now. The paintings, it turned out, were created by employees in a class offered by the hospital. Yes, you heard me correctly. Doctors and nurses and technicians and gurney-drivers – all creating art.

In our car, I pondered this place full of frightened people. And people trying to make them less frightened. That's it, isn't it? That's what a hospital really is. And this isn't intended to be an advertisement for Duke, just my observation. Any large organization can lose sight of what's important. Or it can decide from the top down to be what it should be – loving, kind and as gentle as possible. Beautiful.

"Inspiration is for amateurs" - June 2017

So says Stephen King, the workhorse model of American letters. I am not ashamed to admit that if I could have anyone's – any author's – ethic, it would be his. I don't need to interview him to know this, either. "Get up and plow the field," his output clearly states. If you want to be a writer, *write*. You don't have to like his style, his genre, the books themselves. I don't think I would want to delve into the darkness he has plumbed. But you can't deny that if you write a lot, and read a lot, and have a secure connection in your synapses between what you read and what you write, something will come of it. And, inevitably, your work will get better as you proceed.

Some time ago I was in a writing group – I've told you about the fellow who achieved great first paragraphs and received all of the recognition he required of writing from the writing group's gushing praise for his ideas and initial forays. When we broke up, about seven years ago, there were only two of us still in the game, still writing. Pushing the big lumpy rock up the hill no matter how many times it uses gravity and meanness to roll over us and return to the bottom of that hill. She – my writing group cohort – is the epitome of getting the job done. She produces ideas, outlines, research files, drafts and final product with the regularity of a…no, that's not fair. She's the person that the writing simile should be designed around. And me. I sit every day at the keyboard and type. This and that. On good days and bad.

An editor friend recently received a scathing response from a customer for whom he was providing paid and skilled assistance. *You've badmouthed my characters!* the note stated. *How dare you? Please go F#$K yourself.* My friend asked me if all writers are similarly high-strung. Yes, I replied, gulping. But we're not all quite so bat-shit crazy, so there's that.

My suspicion is – based on no medical evidence whatsoever and intending no coincidental disrespect – that there is a behavioral spectrum for writers. On one end are the working writers who lay down sentences like bricklayers mortaring walls – square, level and practical. I know writers like this and I read their work and I do not attribute the word "art" to their articles and I expect that they do not care what I attribute to their work. Did they do the job assigned? Did they get paid? Done and done.

Moving along the spectrum there are the folks who write, get published, like the work they've done, are aware that it isn't literature, but harbor the secret wish that it was. That is, they wish they could produce better sentences. They keep this feeling close, and it is a part of their personality - a writer's mood, if you will. Perhaps they talk about writing over coffee or cocktails and they are not shy about the work they've produced, but don't brag, either. A little further on are the working writers who are certain that they have that piece of literature in their desk drawer (or up in the cloud, to modernize the image,) but it isn't quite done, not ready, or has been bounced once or twice and they're a tad worried it won't see the light of day without…self-publishing. Yikes!

Along the line are the self-publishers who happily market their wares, the self-publishers who mope, the scribes who don't much care about publishing at all but write for the catharsis or fun or to clear their heads, the happy people who only write when they're in the mood, and those others who are never in the mood, but are patiently waiting to become moody. And on the far end of the spectrum are those who believe that they should only put pen to paper when they are divinely or otherwise inspired.

And, somewhere along this crooked line is my friend's disgruntled customer, the angry scribbler. Do I understand taking things personally? You betcha. Not so recently, but there was a time. *Don't make fun of my poetry. No, I'm not open to advice or correction. Yes, I meant to say that.* So I want to make it clear that in no way am I looking...sideways at any of the personalities of which I speak. Just as it takes a village to make a village, it requires a special kind of tool to be a writer and write. Sometimes that tool comes in a really colorful case. Sometimes the writer finds it difficult to take it out and wield it.

We are hampered and crippled and haunted, encouraged and motivated, each according to our turn. Some days are better than others, of course. My office is in the dining room of our house. Not exactly a quiet corner of my world, with a window out into the pastoral springtime to motivate my creative juices to flow. That it's well-lit and close to the coffee maker is about all I can say about it. At night, when everyone else is down for the duration, it's a good spot for getting things done. So, inspiration or hard work? The cuckoo clock ticks unobtrusively from one wall. My keyboard click-clacks in counterpoint, like Buddy Rich warming up on the snare.

And he would be the first one to tell you that you get to Carnegie Hall by taking the number 4 train and by having correct change for the turnstyle.

Vocabulary Lesson, Day 1 - July 2017

Interesting word problem - is healthcare a *right* or a *privilege*?

I suppose that this depends on what you think rights are, have been, or should be. - all good questions. I think that "privilege" and "right" might be difficult words to use in a critical discussion. They are fraught with political baggage – seemingly simple words which in the past were used to communicate clear messages now wrapped inexorably in agenda and opinion.

Or were they? Were these and other words like them *ever* clean, crisp concepts with universally agreed-on definitions? Did Samuel and John Adams – second cousins and contemporary firebrands of liberty – ever disagree on the finer points of jumping out of Britain's nest? I think that they did.

And how much does *where you've been* determine *where you're going* in such discussions? (My guess on this one – a lot.)

So while I had imagined a short essay explaining (mansplaining? Ugh!) what I think about *critical discussion*, using the healthcare debate as my focal point: how we are better served understanding that healthcare is a *requirement* and we need a healthcare safety net and why planning for an unknown future is elementary school logic and how healthcare providers are professionals and need to be financially rewarded for their skills and sharing that cost is thus and such and so on, as my wise daughter says, I've wandered off into the analogy weeds.

Because it's all just words and we're all tired of them.

Wait, what? Tired of words? When did this happen?

I heard recently (somewhere, out there in the weeds) that most of the communicating done on Facebook will be some form of video. And Facebook is the wave of the future. Right? No?

Maybe it is and maybe it isn't. Maybe Twitter is the wave of the future. The reduction of discussion to its core 144 characters. Reduction of critical analysis to the very kernel. Shrinking of thinking.

My guess, however, is some iteration of Snapchat. The picture that tells a thousand words. Only these pictures are the happy-snaps pointed randomly out into the fleeting reality of giggly preteens. Not to disparage our youth, or anyone's youth, but, whoa. I mean, like, you know? Or is the winner Instagram – which allows those same vapid photos to exist, but for a shorter timeframe. Images with disposable value. ...worth a thousand wor....

Anyhow, it is moot (which doesn't mean a point not worth arguing, but actually the opposite of that. Holy crap, you guys) because the inventions and apps keep coming faster and more furiously at us, in order to take from us that part of us which is valuable – our time – by selling us a bill of goods. Without actually saying it, offering a promise that they can make us more productive. More useful. More youthful. More...something.

But, time being of an essence, let's return to healthcare, if only because I think the conflict there is about words, and definitions of words and interpretations of definitions and what they mean to us because of what each one of us has experienced. In other words (yes, well, sorry), I suspect that most of the difficulty we have with comprehending *community* is in our language – the words we choose and how we use them. Privilege versus right, socialism versus spreading costs, health tax versus proportional premiums. It is the language, might I say even those words specifically, and others, that cause confrontational behaviors, make many folks heels-dug-in intransigent about their point of view regarding healthcare. They feel that their opinion is not respected. And once we are in the mood for digging in our heels – rejecting any future discussion out of hand because we feel we are being condescended to - we tend to lose sight of the actual goal. Which, looking back up the page, was, ahem, to not be so sick anymore.

And herein lies my conclusion. As we take the act of communicating and radically, capriciously, alter it – replacing essays with videos, taking words and using them differently than they were defined, intentionally taking them in a new direction for which they were not designed, we create a deeper divide between ourselves. Or wider, I'm not sure which. We don't make sense to each other. We become, to paraphrase the old chestnut, a people divided by a common language. And when we let this happen and at first laugh it off as silly, as part of our culture of disposable humor, we do ourselves damage. We inadvertently commit to *double-down* on the problem.

Except, ironically, that is not what double-down means.

Magnificent Anachronism - September 2017

I have a summer cold. It's just one of those things, but I have to admit that because I associate colds with winter, it's probably troubling me more than it should. I've just taken cough medicine with codeine, and you may read into that what you will.

I'm not alone when it comes to finding anachronisms akin to literary fingernails on a chalkboard. But I do suspect that we're a small club, not particularly chatty with one another and all behind on our dues. I understand. Anachronism just doesn't occur to everyone as something needing attention.

Let's define it, shall we? Here's what pops up in a general online search: *a thing belonging or appropriate to a period other than that in which it exists, especially a thing that is conspicuously old-fashioned.* Well, first of all that seems almost deliberately obtuse. And by that, I mean wrong. For a thing to be an anachronism, it must be unable to belong in the period in which it exists. So it must, by all logic, not be "conspicuously old-fashioned," but the exact opposite of that – a new-fashioned thing that cannot be there. Like a fleeting glimpse of a Casio wristwatch on a child waving at the 54th Massachusetts Volunteers marching into Savannah in one of my favorite movies.

There is a cottage industry collecting snippets of video of all of the continuity errors, technical flubs, wandering grips and gaffers and time-and-place errors in the history of Hollywood. The implication being that at least a few folks actually have a grasp of what does and doesn't belong historically in a movie and they like the humorous results. And some take their business very seriously. Umbrellas in ancient Troy and kilts in 13th Century Scotland (I didn't know that one. Hell, none of us knew there was a Scotland until the 1950s Gene Kelly movie *Brigadoon*, which is probably Gaelic for trousers, anyhow.)

But the truth is that movies suffer under the withering eye of historical accuracy, because that's not even why they exist. If it can't be told in two hours, scrap it. If it can't be told to a wide audience, scrap it. And editing a movie to prevent Leonardo DiCaprio's Howard Hughes from ordering chocolate chip cookies in 1928 is expensive. I mean *yikes* expensive. Sorry, Toll House…

Writers, on the other hand, have no such excuse. They inhabit a world of their own creation – even if they choose a real world, with real history and timeline and details. There is no committee that has to approve what their characters say, what they do and where they go. So an anachronism is unforgiveable?

No, don't be silly. It's just a mistake.

But for me, the student of both writing and history, it's…off-putting. The problem is, however, that discussing them is a perfect example of getting your panties in a wad. People who don't know history well, and therefore don't much care about the error, think you're an

- A. Know it all.
- B. Jerk, for trying to spoil it.
- C. A bit of an ass who finds some fault in everything.

And that's a problem, because they're all…ahem…true. Or at least partially (read substantially) true. But it's not my fault. Someone has to be that person who fixes mistakes.

Here are a couple of examples that have crossed my Christian Hulsmeyer invented (based on study and research by Heinrich Hertz from seminal work on electromagnetism by James Clerk Maxwell) radar.

I was reading a pretty good book about an alternative mid-20th century history. Don't even get me started on what kind of goat-rodeo you create when you have pertinent smoking-gun details in an alternative history (in the subset of speculative fiction, it is the strange, backwards trousers wearing cousin to science-fiction. Ahh, but I love it so...) because once you break the timeline with a "what-if" you have to suspend your planar thinking that many seemingly unrelated changes are also probable as well as possible. Anyway, in this volume it was the 1930s, and a major character was on a ship and feeling sea-sick, and took Dramamine. The alarum of curiosity went off in my head. Dramamine wasn't invented in the 1930s. It existed, but not for motion sickness. And I looked it up. Bingo. Late 1940s.

Why on Earth, you may ask, would you look *that* up? Who cares when Dramamine was invented? And worse, just shut up, because you're ruining the story for me.

I'm sorry, but there's a point here, and of course and unfortunately it requires a bit of explanation. Did you know that Lord Nelson (the British admiral who fought the French in the Napoleonic wars) suffered from seasickness? If you've ever been even a little bit seasick, you will know that this had to have an effect on his...cognitive reasoning during difficult situations, just as migraines had an effect on George Patton. T. E. Lawrence (Lawrence of Arabia) suffered from motion-sickness riding camels. And there was no good medicine for all of the men on ships on June 5th, 1944, in the English Channel storm just before D-Day, any more than there was a medicine for the Spanish army in the Armada in 1588.

How did I know about Dramamine? Or, better yet, why did I care? Because Pop didn't have Dramamine (or scopolamine, before it was branded) available to him when he needed it to fly home from Guam in '46, and, boy, did that change his life. Hat-ed flying from that moment onward.

If you have some spare time, give scopolamine or hyoscine a *google*. Made from Deadly Nightshade. First written up in 1881. Lots of important uses. Lots of scary side-effects. But on the World Health Organization's list of essential medicines. It's also called the most dangerous medicine in the world. Holy crap. Kind of cool.

Anyhow, a major character can't solve a problem with a solution that doesn't yet exist. It was intended as a nice concrete detail, but it went wrong in the application.

So what? you ask. So it's off-putting to me. What's the big deal with such a minor mistake?

I guess my point is *who's reading historical fiction?* People who ask "what's the big deal about not knowing your history?" Or people who want me to find the mistakes and bring them to their attention.

Or some third set in the Venn Diagram that I haven't even considered, because I was busy taking cough medicine. Yeah, that's a possibility, too.

Oh, shut up, will you?

Here's what I think is one problem. October 2017

You cannot in one breath be complaining about the appalling behavior of men towards women and in the next breath be grousing about whether or not the half and half in your *mochaccino* is organic. You can't go from reading an article about the President signing a bill banning funding to planned parenthood to studying the pending Oscar nominations. From mourning a shooting to a new fortune made playing Powerball. I think no one's brain works like that, at least not well.

In fact, I suspect we are teaching our brains to not work. We are teaching them to play, for lack of a better word. When the newscasters inform us about a bus going over a cliff in India and immediately leap to the weather and giggle about the chance of snow, our brains reach two conclusions – that the first tragedy, while awful, wasn't actually so tragic and that all tragic events can be laughed away if only we can find a lighthearted bit of froth from which to sip.

Coincidentally, I was told a few (well, more than a double-handful) of years ago that people tend to stop being able to learn anything new after the age of forty-five. I don't know why that was the magic age – perhaps the coincidence was that I was on or about my forty-fifth birthday and this tid-bit of information was coming from my sister and she was just informing me that I was starting to become more of a jerk than usual and needed to head this trend off at the pass. Those of you who know me must agree that this explanation seems plausible. In any case, let's go with forty-five. I do know folks who've gone off to get an MBA, or take the deaconate path to the ministry, or been handed the reins to a literary magazine with no experience (ahem), and they were able to learn new stuff. I also know that some folks will just ride in the rut of their situation as if it were an historical imperative. Why one group finds it possible to change horses in midstream and the other to barely change socks each morning is a mystery. It cannot just be some sort of random number, or an actuarially determined age like 25 is for drivers and 65 is for retiring. Can it?

That last paragraph sounded shrill, like an old man muttering in resentful arrogance. My apology. Sometimes the center cannot hold. Maybe I'm going to become that guy. I hope not.

In any case, I'm way past forty-five years of age. I'm reading Japanese novels. Not in Japanese, although that would be quite something. I'm also learning about the life of Martin Luther. And attempting to memorize the sheet music of a Schubert *Valse* so that I can play flute in a duet with my daughter, although there is no telling how that might turn out. And I'm studying how to set up an Access database, breed Platies, make a flan, write a screenplay treatment, track a financial report. And I'm listening to Miles Davis' "Kind of Blue" over and over. Not just a good idea, but a great one.

Why? Why isn't it enough to muddle through with the rest of the planet, bringing my own broom to the noisy rubble of the 24-hour news cycle? Why don't I just walk the dog with a poop-bag in my pocket or take one in the slats with a whiffle-ball bat? Skid downhill on my fanny. Binge on all the TV, and sip cocktails and giggle and snort when the host kicks over his drink? Subscribe to Lawn Edging Illustrated?

Mostly, because I do not want to go gently (or otherwise) into that good night. No, of course I've no way of assuring that I'm not going to slip a cognitive cog. I may assume all I like that since no one in my family is crazy (ha!) that I'm pretty well covered on that account, but the truth is the truth and in my experience it reveals itself as it chooses, almost like a petulant child. But I can do a little bit of arithmetic, and it's high time to get on my horse, take a turn on the crank and learn something else.

Something new.

Thirst – November 2017

Alright, I've been giving a lot of thought to this. I have an entire drawer in the kitchen full of refillable water bottles, with the goal of not buying bottled water from the store. Logical and frugal, right? But here's the thing: once upon a time, I didn't carry around water. I lived in a place called a town, where I had a dwelling called a house (or an apartment, or a dorm room). I went from task to task, and when I felt the oncoming urge to sip at water, because the saliva in my mouth had turned to cotton, or when a headache came on and I needed to ingest a couple of aspirin, I found a restroom or a water fountain or I went home into a room called a kitchen and turned on the tap and let the flow of water fill a glass, then I drank it and relieved this urge to sip. If I was playing outside, say a rousing hand of whiffle-ball or home-free-all, and that need to sip came over me, I called "Time-Out!" and ran to my house to do that drinking-a-glass-of-water thing all over again. Like I hadn't done it just a couple of hours earlier!

Frustrating? No, not really. If I didn't want to run all the way home, I asked a friend if we could go get a glass-of-water at his house. If he didn't want to go all the way inside, we might turn on the outside spigot and drink from the hose! I'm not proud of that, but they were tough times. And if no one wanted to take a time-out for some water, I might just say "OK, see you tomorrow!" and go home to imbibe in a couple of glasses of water. Maybe even with a plunk of ice!

Here's what I imagine: a bunch of old men in the late 90s (the era, not their ages, although you never can tell) in rumpled, expensive suits, sitting around a table thinking about the sort of things such bitter people do.

"Hey," one of the old farts pipes up. "Try this one on for size: if we bottle the water, everyone can just keep on doing whatever they were doing. More productivity because of shorter breaks, right?"

"We've already done that, Fitzwalter, you idiot," growls a wizened little insect-gnome of a man in a tall leather chair. "Too many people stand around the water cooler already!"

"No, no! That's the beauty of this," Fitzwalter the Idiot replies. "First, we convince them with advertisements and celebrity endorsements that they need to take a sip of water all the damned time. I don't know, let's put a stake in the ground and call it 'wetting.'"

"No – that's too much like our adult diaper campaign, whines the ancient gnome.

"What about 'hydrating'" one of the others shouts.

Fitzwalter points a yellowed fingernail at him excitedly. "Even better. And we'll put their water in individual containers at each desk, so they don't have an excuse for getting up!"

"Won't they just drink the bottle up and leave it behind?" asks the gnome-man.

"Not at all, sir. We'll convince them through…medical testimonials, that gulping down water causes cramps, especially when they're really hot or thirsty."

"We have medical testimonials?"

"Not yet, sir. But we will."

A fourth gentleman, younger than the others but just as cold around the eyes, holds up his hand, tentatively. "What if, and I'm just spitballing here, we sell the water to them, as…I don't know…spring water. We'll get the boys in marketing to work up an explanation for how it's even better for them."

Croaks of "Oh, sir! Genius, by god! Pure genius!" and a spattering of applause from the others. Everyone lights up a victory cigarette and they disappear in the billowing smoke like Pompeii beneath Vesuvius.

So I am returning to my youth. I don't carry around water, and yet nothing in my life goes on without me taking a water break. I stop and go to the sink. And when I'm thirsty, I'll gulp a whole glass of water, too. Just try and stop me.

Focus – December 2017

Sometimes the clutter of living gets so deep and snarled that it entwines my path and I can't find the way through.

A sentence so fraught as that can mean only one thing: I have a touch of writer's block. It happens to every writer. OK, maybe it didn't affect Isaac Asimov, but the rest of us mortals stumble into that briar patch from time to time. For me, *the block* manifests itself in a way that is both insidious and ludicrous – the blank page presents so many options that I cannot focus. Friends - writers and not - tell me that this seems a very good problem to be faced with, but to me it doesn't seem so.

Here's how it works, or doesn't so much, depending on your point of view: I begin my day with a file open, a project ready to begin or continued. And I do - *I do* - type away like a busy little shoemaker's elf at the story, the essay, the chapter. But my brain doesn't play well with others. It runs ahead, faster than I can type. It stops staying focused on the sentences rolling off my fingers and throws out what it thinks is a funny punch line to a joke in a story that hasn't been written. A punch line that might work well with a different passel of characters in a different setting than the one I'm currently cobbling within.

Maybe what I get it is better named "writer's flu."

Of course what I need to do is *keep going*, bulldog my way past the compelling, competitive creative noise. What I do, however, is stop, find my composition book – the one with the well-worn cover and the pencil lodged between the leaves, and open it to a blank spot on a page, take the pencil and scribble down the thought. Then I try to find the context that it needs so that when I return to that page, I'm not baffled as to why I wrote down the words "disaster means bad star," or "*imposter complex* is what all students suffer at Harvard." And, no, I don't have magic fingers that can write in italics. I must put big swirling circles around the key words so that I will see them at some point later – when I don't have a clue. If I'm feeling peculiarly lucid, I will date my notes – 10/03/17 – because, why not? Archivists at some vague point in the future will want to know when I lost my mind, right? (Probably not.) A more curious person might ask why I don't keep my notes in order, or why I don't keep them online, or at least in a Word file.

And the answer is I don't know.

Occasionally the new idea decides that it takes precedence over everything; that morning's task, any errands I must run, how well I plan that evening's supper for the girls. It doesn't become a "rabbit-hole," per se, but something closely related to that family. Certainly the new idea has no business thinking this, but that doesn't seem to matter. A new idea is sometimes impertinent; imagines itself precocious, in the classic sense of that term – the young one who imagines itself mature. And so I sit and fiddle with the words, like someone digging post holes for the fence they haven't even drawn a picture of for the spouse to see and agree to, stirring the paint for the first coat, buying workout clothes on January 2nd. I find myself performing all sorts of out-of-order (and mixed-metaphorical) tasks. When I again look up half the day is gone, the sun is past the yardarm. Then I get angry with the new idea, as if it were a puppy that piddled on the Sunday *Times* before I had a chance to pull out the crossword puzzle.

All of which helps not a whit. The new idea is also selfish. If you don't pay it its due, it spins in circles, now a full-grown dog that can't figure out which direction to lie in to sleep. It rolls around in my head like the marbles in the ceiling in Mr. Roberts.

Only they're really there, not like Ensign Pulver's idle promises.

Damn it. See what I mean? Off the rails again. I want to get to work on a writing task, and stay on that task, until it is finished. I want to work through plot problems, polish my prose, create something...elegant. And then I want someone to read it.

Not just anyone, mind. I want my father to read what I write. Dad was my guy, my go-to audience, to see if my funny works, my adventure is breathtakingly real, my sorrow...sorrowful. Was what I was done with ready, reliable, readable. Dad was the person for whom I've been writing, all these years. He could tell me what worked, what he didn't like (curse words put him off a little – he would tell me that I should try harder to find the...creative phrases that could take their place). A lot of folks won't believe this – they cannot imagine a relationship between father and son that isn't tragically confrontational or broken. I was lucky in that regard, even though I don't believe in luck. Things are what you make them, he would say; what you let them become, through action or inaction. He didn't always like what I wrote, but my dad liked that I write. He liked baseball, wine, fishing, singing in the choir, doing crossword puzzles, eating peaches and reading.

And so it is no coincidence that I've been in a bit of a tailspin (talespin?) for a year and change, because that's how long it's been since Dad passed. You couldn't ask for a better reader, he was full of enthusiasm and commentary. All writers suffer from writer's block occasionally. I'm not sure how many suffer from readers' block. But he would say, "get back to work," and so I do.

Almanac Entry – January 2018

It's 64 degrees Fahrenheit in our living room – because I'm stubborn, mostly, and also because no one else is home at the moment and I don't need it to be particularly warm to type here. (It's cooler outside, but still November-ish sunny and I'm considering changing venues for writing this document.) I have a cup of tea - cream and sugar, thanks - and it's helping me maintain appropriate body warmth. I have a sweatshirt on, also, but the sleeves are rolled up, figuratively and literally. Today has been a very good day.

It started off iffy enough. (I like that last sentence a lot. Say it out loud, three times, fast.) For reasons I cannot easily comprehend, although "tired" leaps to mind, I went to bed at 7:30 last night. Fell almost immediately asleep, woke up ridiculously early this morning and got to work. I'd thought I would read – I mean really read, for a few hours. Serious, uncompromising consumption of text, like so many folks I know say (on Twitter of all things) that they are able to do. "I blasted through that book this weekend. No kidding, man, you just have to *reeeeead* it!"

Other than the unnerving feeling I have that the dialogue above seems excavated from a dim and crusty tomb from 1978, what I'm thinking right now is that I rarely have the opportunity to lay track like that, end to end. Something always trips and falls in the way. The phone, meals, laundry, someone needing a ride somewhere. Someone needing a ride home from somewhere. Someone wanting something off a high shelf. (How do things get on those high shelves, anyhow? It's not me, is it? I don't think it's me.)

The world conspires against reading, and by direct association, writing. Society is interruptive by nature. Interruptions always take precedence. We not only let them, but we seem to embrace permitting them to unhorse us from our appointed tasks. We are motivated to look at our phones, at the news, at the weather, to ensure that we think we know what's going on right now.

I recently received a rejection notice from a publishing house to which I had submitted a novel, intended for the YA audience. They were very efficient and forthright. And kind, by the way. One reason, they admitted, for not selecting the piece for publication was that I spent too much time at the start of the thing developing the character and setting. My storytelling did not immediately get down to business. As you all know, this function of writing is referred to as *in media res*, which is Latin for "just before the bomb goes off." Sam Spade's lovely young thing pitching a mystery at the door of his office was chapter two. Chapter one was some poor slob being pitched from a moving train.

Back in the day, I was taught that this was just one option of many for an aspiring author. If you wanted, you could always spend a little time getting to know Odysseus and his family, or the Spartan king and his pretty new wife, Helen, rather than having Achilles spearing some giant Arcadian in the shoulder in the first paragraph, although that sure would have grabbed your ancient Greek *therapeia* (attention!) And if it seemed they were going into a lot of detail about who and where and when and why, it's because there were only three books in the whole world and the *Iliad* was one of them and the *Odyssey* was another and we think the third one was about some hunter fellow named Gilgamesh. So there was something to be said about having a semi-captive audience to your narrative stylings. It took a young short story writer named Moses to come up with that pithy phrase "In the beginning…" and launch a heck of a yarn about sin and redemption. But even his prose contained a fair bit of miraculous window-dressing before it settled down to spinning a coming-of-age story.

Speaking of coming-of-age, if we but leap forward a few centuries or so, we find the first lines of a saga where Our Hero is described by the poet as a baby! What is the point of that? Is the baby even doing anything...Herculean? Nope. Just being named and catalogued. And that's the whole point. We know the story, we even know how it ends. We don't just want to see the baby, either. We want the labor pains. We ought to demand the thing, warts and all. If some *scop* is going to stand up and shout "Hear Me!" after a big meal and a lot of drinking, and even knowing that it's an oldie but a goody like Beowulf, well, starting at the very beginning whets our appetite for a good long winter's tale.

My point is Gone With the Wind doesn't begin with the burning of Atlanta. Catch-22 has no bombings on the first page that I recall. War and Peace launches not in the middle of a battle, for crying out loud, but rather a very personal struggle for place at the grownups' table, and a fair amount of French that you need to look up on the footnotes page. Anyhow, there is much to be said for getting to know people before you put them in harm's way.

There are rules for writing a novel, but no one knows what they are, to paraphrase another Somers(et Maugham) type. Or maybe they're not rules, but...aspects of narrative that readers are currently in the mood for. But if all stories start out the same way – then how do we differentiate between them? The level of immediate excitement? The increasing violence or terror or sex or other fascination-factor splashed onto the page by an ever more exhausted author stable trying to please a jaded, slippery-sloped readership? Perhaps.

Perhaps not.

Maybe I'll try again, tonight. I've a lot of very good books on the nightstand. By the way, my daughter is reading King's "It." She's on chapter three. Tells me she's a little bit bored because right now it's all about adults. She asks me if they all kill themselves. I sigh. You're on page fifty of a thirteen-hundred page novel, sweetie. Give it a chance.

Talking with young writers – March 2018

Never miss an opportunity. If your grandpa is going to fry chicken after church – don't sleep in. Get out of bed and clip on that tie and go to service. Afterwards, grab yourself a thigh and an ear of corn and some butter-beans and dig in.

No, it's not new advice. We let things slip by us too often, I think. Imagine ourselves exhausted - just frazzled, worn down to the bone. I get it, I really do. You're tired of the grind, and the rancor that surrounds the grind like a clinging miasma. You just want to do what you must, and when it's done or over get back inside without getting too dirty, sit in your chair, watch your shows or flip through your postings and then sleep. Wake and do it all again. If opportunity knocks, maybe if you're quiet, it won't bother you. Some other time, perhaps. *Not right now.*

Opportunity isn't a robo-caller that will keep annoyingly dialing until you answer. It passes like a comet; once in a while, or not at all. Never often enough for us to lose our curiosity in what caused the moment – all possibility and flash with a valuable prize at the core. But sometimes curiosity and laziness, like a sad cocktail bordering on despair, are a tough scale to tip.

And just in case you're thinking that it's easy for me to say this, because I'm _____ (fill in the blank with whatever hyperbole you use as a measure of success) well, I know of what I speak. I am a notorious non-attender. And not just things most of us don't like to do (like going to the DMV or grocery store or to get a haircut, but good things, too!) What they now generally name *social anxiety*, I have in double-handfuls. Would I like to go to a birthday party? I would. How about an extra concert ticket – would I like it? You bet. Meet up for dinner? Indeed.

But as time marches on between the invite and the event my eagerness wanes, passing like a pop-up thunder-boomer with sound and foolery but not much in the way of useful rain or cooling temps, so that the idea of actually tripping the light semi-fantastic percolates in my sad little brain into pre-regret, and any actual enthusiasm withers like honeysuckle in a drought. In the end, only guilt or a not-so-gentle nudge gets me out the door.

I volunteer at my local elementary school, where I am a judge for their annual Young Authors program. The elevator-pitch on this is that every student is invited to write a book in any genre, including short story and poetry collections. They have the entire fall to do so, and the teachers assist with helping understand the difference between "realistic fiction" and non-fiction, and how to write a bio-sketch.

The program has been going on for over 25 years – I swear! – and shows no sign of age (and not just because new children arrive each to fill in the spaces left by everyone moving up one grade.) It is a very cool thing how much support the school has for writing and how enthusiastic the kids are to put their creative minds to paper. By the way, we give a small award to the Young Author in the fifth grade who we think did a terrific job on their book.

And in the end, after everything is written and illustrated and covered and bound (and judged) there is a Young Authors Tea. Everyone attends. Awards are distributed. And who's hurt by a little Chex Mix, juice boxes and applause? No one, say I. It is a good thing.

This year, near the end of the awards ceremony, the head of the program had each student who had written a book but hadn't won an award stand up anyway to be recognized. More applause!

And then it was my turn to give the award. I took the mic and I spoke - social anxiety and all.

I told the kids, and the teachers and parents, that while it is a fine thing to be recognized, what happened this fall - writing a book - wasn't *participating*. That was the wrong word. What they did was "accomplish." And that there is a big difference. They got something done. They wrote a book. And if they can write a book, well, they can write another book. Because writing is not about winning or losing – it's all about telling a story – getting the tale out of your head and onto the page. Then I gave the award (a gift certificate to a local Indy bookstore, of course) to a girl who'd written a perfectly original, surprising and fresh, fable.

On my way back to my seat, one of the teachers whispered "Bravo!" to me as I passed.

In the end I like a good game of solitaire as much as the next person. I use the version that comes with the operating system on my computer when I am sitting and thinking about what is going to happen next in a story I am writing. It is perfectly fine white noise for the creative mind. But life is not solitaire. Not a productive life. Not a fine, fun life. You have to take your cards next door and see if your neighbor plays…I don't know, *cribbage*.

And so I (purport to) go. I know, or at least I think I know, the difference between diffidence and unwillingness to take the bull by the horns. That's way of the world.

In other words, no matter how grim and grimy life may seem from time to time, and in the gloomy months of a new year, it is its grimiest and grimmest, you need to get up and do what needs doing. Even if there is no fried chicken at the end. With butter-beans.

The Four-Minute Coffee Symphony – April 2018

They say coffee lowers your chances of developing cirrhosis of the liver. It is a strange sentence with unfortunate word choice, because by saying "lowers" rather than "reduces" a reader might assume that one wants a higher chance of developing cirrhosis of the liver. They – a completely different *they* as far as I know, say that the caffeine in coffee and the milk-fat in half-and-half and the sugar in sugar puts a great big *meh* in your libido. OK, actually it was me that used the phrase "*meh* in your libido" but that's because I'm uncomfortable talking about anatomy.

And I don't know who *they* are, and not knowing puts a really dull edge on the point I'm trying to make because it could be that my hypothesis is built on a troll, and depending on how you define troll - nothing has been done like that since either 7:45 this morning or in a story told to either one of the brothers Grimm, that is Jacob and Wilhelm (also known as Rumpelstiltskin) back when they wandered the Upper Palatinate trying to come up with a new way to harvest rye or join the Bavarian Army as ad-hoc farriers - your morning cuppa has been…tainted.

That was one heck of a sentence, wasn't it?

My suggestion – never read, watch, scan, check or listen to anything before your coffee. Talk? Yes. Gaze? You betcha. Scroll? Unless it's something you found in the wreckage of the library at Alexandria, best to play it safe and ignore said electronic parchment until after you've hit dregs.

I think what actually happens after your Joe is that coffee speeds up your actual space-time continuum until you're going at 45 or even 78 revolutions per minute when the rest of the world is at 33 & 1/3. I am reliably informed that the medico-technical term for this is "zoom." Effectively, you live the same life-span and do many of the same things – respond to e-mail blasts, curb your appetite, binge-watch "Stranger Things," consume the *Decline and Fall of the Roman Empire*, only with much greater celerity, so that in the end your life seems way longer.

And speaking of celerity, auto-correct keeps trying the following words out on me as alternatives to what I already know I meant: celebrity, celery and calorie. No, no and no. Thanks for playing, Silicon Valley, California, programmers, and it's still your turn.

It is also, so far, so that under espresso's very much not so-so (hee!) influence I have a better chance of finding rhymes to various word choices for the schemes I select in the doggerel I like to pen in my writers' journal while sitting on my front porch watching the neighbor mow his lawn. I am peculiarly fond of this activity, because it uses three of the five basic laziness groups: sitting, watching and brainstorming. Based on this, in our house we are renaming the fifth day of the week "Thesaurusday." Please feel free to celebrate this in your own home, suggesting to your kids that they must come up with three verb-subject-object alternatives to the interrogative "may I play World of Warcraft now?" before you will relinquish the iPad. Also, it won't hurt anyone if they first have to play "international rules tag-team vacuuming." Note to self: you've put the two words in the English language with double-Us (not W's) in your essay. You may now die a happy scribe!

Regarding libido - the subject that no one wants to talk about but it's already out there and how can we avoid thinking about it even if we don't *talk* about it (go ahead, try to not think about it!) there are so many other things to blame and using Occam's Razor (which should always be used even when the concepts of male performance and razors do not combine well in the old Venn diagram, no, not well at all) it is more probable that any of the current socio-political discussion streams is more likely to make you want to go hide in a cave and no that is not a thinly-disguised metaphor.

Anyway, as you go about your daily thing, your body, preparing to begin its cirrhosis of the liver phase, so to speak, performs an end-run around the ailment and crashes headlong into the other vehicles in the parking lot called death. And I'm not going to tell you that life is short, and that what you ingest is harmless, although for the most part it is, as long as you chain yourself to a big, big rock before ingesting gamma rays or any kind of hallucinogenic pharma. So eat a burger, pink on the inside. Have another mug of Breakfast Blend. What the hell. You're going outside to fight giant insectoids from *Klendathu*, for crying out loud.

Of course, I've had a couple of cups of French Roast this morning and could be wrong, but I'm already working on something else and really don't care.

Poetry Book – May 2018

Eleven years ago, I began scribbling in a blank book. Well, it actually just looks like scribbling because my handwriting, even when I slow down and use a fancy pen and really pay attention to the crafting of each letter, is only borderline-legible. This particular blank book contained the impromptu poetry inspired by sitting in a car (A beige Nissan van) waiting for children to finish. Finish class, karate, a birthday party, gymnastics, what have you. That, however, is not the punch-line of a Dad-joke. Actually, that little blank book was the beginning of a lesson.

Hear me out. I promise, no lecture.

At the time, eldest daughter was in third grade, and youngest was just starting kindergarten. They were both, finally, in the same school, and I was their preferred mode of transport (along with food, clothing, teeth-brushing, face-washing and entertainment coordination.) We passed a lot of time in that old beige van, waiting for traffic to move, school to start, rainstorms to blow over, this or that event to commence. Reading! Listening to a song on the radio. Watching a movie. Snacking on chips and juice-boxes, coloring, drawing, writing poetry. Truth! *Writing poetry*. And my third-grader had reached the point in her education where she decided that she was beginning to understand what poetry actually is.

Far be it for me, at this point (in the story as well as today) to try and encapsulate "what is poetry?" in a 700-word essay. What I did try to do with my daughters is tell them how I felt about a poem, what it was like for me to cobble an image (for at best, I am a shoemaker) and to begin the discussion with them about the difference between a poem and poem-fragment. Poetry is art as much as painting or sculpture. You have to work at it, like a garden that you plant and tend and weed and water. "Is a poem the whole garden, or is it a flower in the garden?" I asked them once, a while ago. Oh, Dad, replied my then-third grader. I thought you meant a vegetable garden. Good point. So, some of my words stuck and some were considered and dismissed. Which, I think, is both good and as good as it gets, perhaps in equal measure.

I know I promised no lecturing, but I used to think that the responsibility for teaching about poetry, the great poets of history and their works, was a great, necessary and wonderful burden that teachers (and parents and authors and editors and other poets) all shared. *This, you see, is good poetry, and this over here? Not so much. Read Gerard Manley Hopkins! Read Yeats and Keats (or is it Kates and Yeets?) You're too young to know what's good for you!* (Hey, Dad! Did you know "groan" is a homonym for "grown?")

And I think I know, if not the precise moment that my mind changed, the two ideas that broke through the calcification. One was a friend's son, who told him that while he respected his father's opinion on some things (like art, politics and career choices) he wasn't going to follow all of his father's advice. Why not? Because he knew what his own interests were, wasn't terribly concerned about making mistakes, anyhow, fifty years from now being wrong wouldn't matter very much because he (Dad) wouldn't be around to say, "I told you so." My friend argued with his son for a while, because that's what fathers do, but always his son returned to the point that in the end, it was his decision.

Damn – that's good. By the way, my friend, rather than pushing back against this rock, has embraced it (his son is wicked smart.) Stop worrying about those things that you cannot change, change the things you can, etc., etc.

But, I tell my own progeny, you don't know enough about poetry, or painting, or drama, or music!

My own daughter's response? "Dad, you're probably wrong about this." Full points for being concise.

So, while I really do think that poetry is the responsibility of those who follow us, what we found to be judged great and wonderful may change, if not for us, for others. Time was our unit of measure. *This poem has been read for a long time, therefore it is good and it must be read by you. You will see for yourself how great it is, and if you don't, I will explain it to you!*

Rubbish. Those marvelous, dusty works may not resonate for them. I mean, they might, but might not. I still put the poems I love in front of her, and the music and art and films and books and, and, and. But I don't bludgeon her with how great they are (much) and I don't dismiss the art she loves. And if my daughters, for example, find poetry in a garden different from mine, who am I to judge them on that? It's their poetry at that point, all that is and all that ever was. Because I will be gone, someday. And they, and others, will hand that sheaf of papers down to the next group of young poem writers and readers. And trust me, I didn't make up this line of reasoning – again, my eldest revealed it to me in her follow-on comment to my *wrongness*.

How, I asked her – not at the time; I never have the correct words when I need them (more's the pity) – will you be certain to give the next generation all the same possibilities to find poetry that…I'm giving you? What I said was "How am I wrong?" (oh, the list of things…)

Easy, Dad, said she. Don't throw anyone or anything under the bus.

I suspect that this sounds preternaturally profound for a third grader. In any case, I have grown up in the ensuing eleven years to find that she was not only right, but that embracing this idea makes things a bit easier. My advice? Throwing people and their art under the bus is a lot of heavy lifting, and nothing good comes of it.

Circadian Arrhythmia – June 2018

Aaron Sorkin (I'm not going to tell you who he is, either you're already well aware and it will be ironic, or you're not and I will be left foolishly mansplaining) said something to the effect of "the first sin of writing is to tell the reader what they already know."

Elder daughter says I talk too much. Sort of the same thing, I guess.

It's late spring, and there are perhaps a handful of lovely cool mornings remaining in the inventory. The alarm pushes me out of bed and downstairs to my keyboard and just before I sit I peer out the window. I have no foolish thoughts that I am the only one awake and the moment is peaceful; outside are the dog walkers, the school bus riders, the running women and men getting cardio, the landscape workers prepping their gas-powered weed-eaters and edgers while checking their watches for that seven-thirty start time.

Across the street is another me, my neighbor who I don't know a thing about except that he likes to sit on his porch and watch the world, our very small slice of it, pass. I'm on my side, he's on his. We claim no right to quiet, to privacy, to…empire. We just sit. He reads, I read. If someone is blowing leaves or mowing the lawn, I go back inside. (I stay out for the stink of steak sizzle on a grill, though. I mean, who doesn't?)

Occasionally we wave hello – or goodbye – to each other, to other neighbors walking by. I wonder what they think of us - two silent, frumpy sirens past whom folks must navigate to go home. I wonder what he's got in his tumbler. I have pineapple-juice and seltzer in mine. Nothing hard, nothing sugary (please don't tell me any truth about pineapple-juice. At least it's better for me than the aeronautic zoom and crash of sweet tea.) And no, I'm probably never going to get up and wander across the street and introduce myself.

One of my favorite things is catching people power-walking while they jabber away on Bluetooth. It is efficient to walk and work, but they seem to be talking to themselves and there is an element of fun to pretending that they aren't. As they pass my perch, I say hi when they say hi. I try to answer questions they ask the person they're on the horn with. My goal, of course, is to earn the stink-eye. It is silly and who couldn't use more silly?

Right now, my autocorrect is trying to get me to change "more silly" to "sillier." I refuse to be bullied.

The days get longer. Dawn cracks at Five fifty-five. Five, fifty-two. Night leaks out of the overturned bottle. Every morning, first light peers over my horizon in shades of watermelon and carnation, lilac and fandango. It's difficult for me to decide if I like spring (because of warmth and rebirth and new bloom) or if it is troubling (because I have to come out of my cocoon, leave my comfortable cave of winter.) Do bears feel this way, I wonder. Or are they just happy to get a meal after a long fast? Along that line, I am not a morning-feed person. In December it feels strange to eat when it's still dark out. By the time warm weather has returned for good, it is still an oddity to me to think about eating breakfast. I do, however, enjoy a couple of eggs over-easy and a rasher or two of bacon before settling down to a long night. This is of course an evil thing to do, cooking up when everyone else is asleep. Their dreams must warp from flying unicorns and magnificent shopping malls to coming down to the feast-perfumed kitchen only to find it empty, or worse – full of dirty dishes.

This morning I grind the beans, prop open the clean, brown, climate-change reversing filter and make the coffee. I put together the tasty lunch for my youngest (not so young anymore, though) and crack the blinds. Crank the desktop like an old flivver. We had a run-in, my computer and I, this year, but with some minor open-heart surgery and a software facelift she's back in fighting trim. I like writing in the morning. It is akin to scrubbing your face with a clean wet washcloth. Get everything out there, on paper, even if it's not much use later. Reveal things. Unclog the pipes, turn the soil over to the day. Yes, I'm fully aware that Victorians defined "soil" differently than I do. Ah, well.

Here in my "office" – the coopted formal dining room of this house – I have stacked my desk with the clutter of failed attempts to focus. ARCs, sketchbooks, shells I picked up on the beach, old bookmarks as weathered and dog-eared as the books they stood watch over for me. No food-crumbs or dirty coffee-cups, though, so points for effort. There are four different chairs at the table, so I can wander around like Isaac Asimov – a new spot for each change-of-project. I turn the monitor and reposition the keyboard and carry on. It's silly, I know, but sometimes you need to be silly to keep going. There's also a terrific wing-chair, leather, in the corner beneath the snick-snocking cuckoo clock. It's a great chair. Not a couch – god, I would lay down to rest my eyes and wake up four hours later and stay up all night (not that this would be particularly terrible, but…) – just a good reading chair.

For those of you keeping count, I stole two references to Julie Andrews' movies in paragraph six. Go back and see if you can find them!

I think I'm pretty fair at drafting (not the thing where you pull your car up on the bumper of the driver in front of you while roaring down the freeway to try and save a couple of pennies of gasoline but plowing the field of a writing project and getting words down) and know all of the hints & tips - don't look back, just keep typing, edit later, etc., and just keep typing. Elementary stuff, but you would be surprised by how many folks keep bunching up their panties with the first paragraph of their story and never finish the damned tale. It's a perfect paragraph, though, so there's that.

Well, my nutritionist says I have to go now, get outside before the heat of the day becomes an excuse for not doing my half-hour of aerobic exercise. Yes, I have a nutritionist, and she's very smart. Doesn't take any clever crap from me. I go out and walk and pretend to be on Bluetooth while I actually talk to myself about schedules and morning sunshine and writing and such. Of course, just when you get a handle on the whole spring thing,

Daylight Savings throws it all into a cocked hat.

Movie Review July 2018

Watched *The Desk Set* again, recently. Sat in front of the "other TV" in our house – a 19 incher we keep upstairs for the poor sap who was outvoted that evening. Often that's me, but OK. The truth is, a small screen is perfect for the playful banter between Kate Hepburn and Spence. He, caught in the rain in his Tracy-fedora, so she invites him in to dry off. Earlier, she, freezing on the roof of a Manhattan office building because he thinks a picnic in, what...October? is a good idea? A ham & cheese sammy and plenty of hot coffee, kid. Hang in there.

Here's where my brain took me: how fun was this, actually? It's good-old 1957, the year of my creation, and people still take scheduled coffee-breaks and rotary-dial their telephones down to a department of sweater- gals with "freshly-scrubbed faces" who answer fun questions about Astrology and the proper temperature for cooling Jello and the lyric poetry of The Love Song of Hiawatha and J. Alfred Prufrock. I don't remember these sort of antics exactly, of course, but there was just a little bit of it, the butt-end of the old-school loaf, say, when I was starting out as a freshly-scrubbed…whatever. Suit and tie. Typewriters. Erasable bond paper! Inter-office memoranda. Company cafeterias with soup-of-the-day.

Just in case you're not familiar with the plot, Tracy is trying to install a "mechanical brain" in this office. That's what they called computers (in Hollywood, because not everyone with a quarter for a movie ticket knew what a computer was, much less what the skyline of New York looked like). An oh-my-gosh, they're taking over our jobs, plot. Sounds vaguely familiar. Very tongue-in-cheek, see, with Hepburn's "Bunny" trying to land a man (Gig Young, who I cannot disconnect from his deep-into-the-disappointed-1970's role as the head of the CIA-like organization that shot James Caan in *The Killer Elite*.) And the post-depression and War world is innocent – I mean we're still three years from Jack Lemmon renting out his so-called apartment so that married boss Fred MacMurray (heaven forfend, it's My Three Sons' Dad!) can boink sweet-drunk Shirley MacLaine someplace other than the back of a Yellow Cab or the Drake Hotel.

Why wasn't that as deeply troubling as it ought to have been? Oh, yeah. Because like the Hepburn/Tracy film, we're still coming to grips with certain beliefs: that women are smart but not quite as…important in the workplace as men. They get jobs, but those jobs are replaceable – by technology! Women need coffee breaks. They can do pretty good work (the men do annual reports, proofread by women.) And, anyhow, doesn't plucky Shirley MacLaine pick herself up, dust herself off and start all over again? Win the guy in the end? So ta-da, right? And even if we reject this point out of hand, how quickly do we forgive the corporate world? Sure! By the following year, J. Pierpont Finch is already succeeding in business without really trying. Hey, it's OK, kids, in movies, using gender as a weapon is Fun! Right?

Right?

But here's where my thinking really wants to go. Fifty-odd years forward. New movie. Similar subject. In this particular flick, it's still the somewhat distant past, IBM is still trying to install a piece of big iron – and the workplace is still having "girl trouble."

The chief characters are the so-called "computers" - the highly skilled and reliable African-American women who work on an assignment basis like contract employees – receiving those very inter-office memoranda to report to this or that department and do the NASA heavy-lifting of *mathematics*. Like secretaries keeping the drunken boss from falling out of his chair and hurting himself on the concrete floor, the computers are human mechanical brains who tote up the columns, double-check the measurements or even do the extraordinary trigonometry to ensure that these manned-missiles don't make, to quote a different space-race film, *spam in a can* out of anyone. Then the computers are placed back in the pool to await their next assignment. Career? No. Job security? Ha! (Remember that mainframe that IBM is installing?) That they are women, and deeply underappreciated for, well, much of a lifetime – *my* lifetime - is one point of the movie. That they are black women is…unexpected. And that this truth is unexpected is shameful. The additional nonsense they must endure at work is inexcusable. And that's not at all funny.

So we're here now, and some things have changed, and other things seem new, but they're not. I can easily imagine Katharine Hepburn's Bunny as the head of marketing, working for a successful internet firm founded by Octavia Spencer's Dorothy. A good place to work, with sensible child-care policies and flexible work-scheduling.

On the other hand, I'm glad I got to work in a big company during a time when they thought equal-opportunity was not just a memo. That I had good managers who were women, or black, or older, or older black women.

And that I, alone it seems, got out before I became age-disposable, and lived to tell the tale.

Addendum:

Ten secret skills I passed on to my daughters during my Stay At Home Dad tenure. (July 2018)

One: Know how to spit. Spitting is a vastly underrated talent – I mean if you can't do it, you're always the spastic one at the beach trying to get windblown sand out of your mouth or looking panic stricken enough for your friends to put you on snapchat that time you inhaled a gnat. There's more to it than puckering up and saying *ptooee*, too. There's inhaling without inadvertently swallowing, rolling up your tongue to create the projectile tube, and then puffing with authority, without making your head do that Hollywood spit-move (as if it would help somehow to get extra momentum from your neck...) And not looking after you've spit. And not wiping your mouth with your hand or shirt-sleeve. Just spitting, like you do it every day. I also taught them how to hock up a loogie, but we frown upon it, because it's showing off. And we don't show off, do we.

Two: Never hold a grudge. Things that are going wrong right now may turn out to be irrelevant in the future, but others aren't so...inclined to forget clever/hateful things you say today. Sure, it's okay to be grumpy with someone for a little while, but then get on in there and tell them you're sorry. Apology is good for you, trying to keep track of your enemies is exhausting. So let whatever it is *go*.

Three: There are many small life-hacks, when you find them, embrace them: Show up early to appointments and on time to parties. Pick up after yourself and other people. Learn to power nap without ruining your night's sleep. If you can't sleep through the night, get up and get things done. Read when you go to the bathroom. Park in the first empty parking place you find and walk. Let your resting-face be a smile. If you have a few minutes, let other people go in front of you at the check-out line. Etcetera, etcetera…. Most of these are just a matter of acquiring "muscle memory" and will stick with you the rest of your life. And you'll be better for it.

Four: Cultivate new hobbies, but don't throw old ones away. The more different things you enjoy doing the more you bring the creative part of you forward, the more interesting you will be, and the more you will have that you can do when you're older. Which you will be, someday, no matter how much you don't believe it.

Five: Help without worrying about return favors, ask for help without worrying about what you owe. Make others feel necessary. Help others accomplish what they cannot accomplish alone.

Six: Whistle while you work. It was just a song when I was little, but it made such sense. Rake leaves, clean toilets, answer the customer support calls, fold the laundry. Bus the tables. Unload the groceries from the car. At least be helpful. At most, understand the value of choosing to do the dirty job that no one else leaps up to volunteer for. No, you never get paid appropriately, but if you can do this one thing, you can do almost anything, cheerfully. And when you are doing the dirty job, no one looks over your shoulder to make sure you're working hard and doing it right. No one will shout at you to hurry up. Why not? Because they don't want to be told "you're so smart, here you go, you do it!"

Seven: Having already acquired skill two, remember to say what's on your mind early and often. Don't hold back until you feel life/school/job/relationship is unfair. And don't suddenly become someone else when your mood changes. Put the person you really are *up front*, opinionated, passionate, always honest and...now shut up and listen to the other person. Look them in the eye. Ask questions about what they're saying, so that they know you're listening and interested in what they have to say. And, if you should, apologize for talking too much.

Eight: Set and meet your goals, but not for rewards other than personal accomplishment or wisdom. Grades, ratings, salaries, recognition is all good, but not the *all-good*. Achieve because it is what you committed to do, and because learning is its own reward. And give yourself a pat on the back for emptying the dishwasher as often as you do for making your...quarterly sales goals.

Nine: It's not how you look, but how you feel about how you look. Take care of yourself, but don't' let anything so fleeting as beauty become an obsession.

Ten: Small victories and small joys. This one is not precisely how it sounds. One should strive for victories but also have/find satisfaction in the small steps of achievement. Learned something new? Good. Read and turned the page? Also very good.

Going out of style – with style! (Indisputably, Part one) – August 2018

Recently I was explaining home ownership to my eldest. This is easily one of my favorite things. She enjoys (sometimes) hearing me talk and likes (always) pulling my chain – often asking the next question before I've finished answering the first. In this particular conversation, however, things deteriorated subject-wise to the point where I was trying to tell her what a mortgage was and how it works, while she was already off on the tangent of renting, then leasing, and then wanted me to clarify the difference between taking out a loan and paying rent, and so on. All this while we stuffed our faces with pork chops and mashed potatoes. It was glorious, because we both knew how boring it was, and yet we continued forward like two crazed individuals rappelling down the side of a mountain, knowing that the rope wasn't quite long enough to reach the bottom.

"Hey Dad," she eventually interjected. "What is the difference between loaning and lending?" And my brain hiccupped, because it was a good question, a scholar's question. But all I could think to say was that *loan* is a noun and *lend* is a verb.

Ahhh, but Google told it differently. A quick search showed they were both words from the old Germanic (with proto-Indo-European roots), origins timed in the fifteenth century. Both have noun and verb uses. It didn't say when they were locked in place with grammatical rules, but I stubbornly reiterated that I was taught that one never says, "can you loan me your car?" but rather, "can you lend me your car?" The car is that thing which we lend. It is the loan (noun). The act of lending it, the verb.

I was also a little surprised that one of the examples given to explain this usage was, "can I have the loan of your car?" which threw it all into deeper, muddier grammatical water. And that "lend" is used more in British English, and "loan" in American English. Why this is so, it didn't deign to say so.

How much of the change, the *evolution* of the words, I asked myself, is due to faulty usage in the first place? Faulty usage that gains traction with so many users that eventually it becomes the new *norm*. And how much to *ease of use*, to economy, where two words that basically mean the same thing (in their root) are beginning to overlap in all functions until they reach synonymity?

And so all I can think is that one of them is going out of style, and the other will eventually be the common usage. I like to imagine that evolution is something that happens so slowly that it's difficult to pinpoint the event and it doesn't upset your personal applecart, but words are excellent examples of items whose comings and goings we can date with some accuracy.

I will tell you right now that I prefer "indisputably" over "undisputedly," if they are traveling down some vague path towards synonymousness. (And I must say that I prefer using synonymousness over synonymity if for no other reason than because if you are a reader who subvocalizes, you're going to stumble a bit there because of all the susurration involved. Hey, if we can't have fun with words, what's the point.)

But here we are hoisted on our own petard, because indisputably and undisputedly are not really synonyms. Not yet, anyhow. Indisputably means that after discussion, we all agree. Undisputedly means that even with no discussion, we all agree. That is what we call in the scribbling business a *clear distinction*. But the writing world is not the real world. When we make mistakes in word choice like this, it means that we don't see the clear distinction. But the point is moot, if we're in evolution mode. And ironically, moot does not mean that the point isn't worth arguing about. It means that the point is worth arguing about (but perhaps we just don't have the time for it, so let's move on.

So words change. I know that, in the bones where I write, but I don't always like the changes, or have to like them but must deal with them. Maybe I'm getting old. Words are meant to be remodeled, tweaked. We are creatures of language, but we are also provincial, no matter how cosmopolitan we claim to want to be. We talk the talk of our neighborhoods and townships, our cliques and clubs. It assists us in belonging, making things comfortable. So betwixt mutates into between. Or maybe they start at around the same era on two sides of the same mountain, and for similar reasons. Expanding, reaching out, they meet somewhere near the middle; the two words that mean the same thing hash it out, like duelists, for supremacy in the lexicon of the new, amalgamated people.

And I also think some mistakes require a society that occasionally takes out its red pen and marks up the copy. Fewer becomes lesser. One person's inadvertent idiocy becomes idiom. Inexplicable inexplicably becomes unexplainable. Some root I cannot even hazard a guess at becomes persnickety, like a twig stepped on in a forest after a tree falls, alone. I've been told that one most common type of linguistic foul-up is called an "eggcorn;" a word or phrase that was passed along misheard, misspelled or misunderstood. A good example is "tow the line" rather than "toe the line." Fun, almost clever, but wrong.

Instinctively (or instinctually – I can no longer say with confidence which), we editors try and make sense of the evolution of language, as it unrolls beneath our stumbling, but comfortably shod feet. Sometimes we get snarled in the mundane barbed wire of *em* dashes or Oxford commas, single or double spacebars after a period, but some of us run on through this no-persons' land to leap into the trench on the other side, only to find that its occupants are no less or more enlightened about whether GIF is pronounced with a hard G or soft J sound. If we're lucky, the disagreements don't come to rancorous tweets filled (inasmuch as 144-character outbursts can be) with smarmy, sardonic wit. And then we are dashed against the stone by apps with no words, only pictures, because they tell a thousand words. Or do they? We hush and carry on. We leave that alone.

There is no check for this kind of change. Grammar police have no teeth. Educators are busy with more critical concerns. Journalists are...surrendering to the mob. The truth is, there is no more expedient way to age than start correcting someone else's use of language. Insist that *google* is not a verb and the massed rolling of eyes will crush you like Sisyphus atop a hill in Hades. Your family and friends will assume that you've lost your ever-lovin', blue-eyed mind. In My Fair Lady, no one likes Henry Higgins. No one. Be honest, he was a bit of a putz. Act like that and people will cease talking in front of you.

They will, however, talk behind you, wink-wink. And, in the end, we wish you good luck, for you cannot edit the entire world as it hyphenates, abbreviates, misspells, misuses, misquotes, misinterprets, takes out of context, acronyms, deafens, italicizes, sub(con)textualizes, dangles, predicates and horsewhips the language into something so vague and mutant in its construct that it is nearly indecipherable. You'll be boiling an unconjugated ocean.

And dinosaurs like me were intended to die out anyway, were they not?

Indisputably, Part two – September 2018

In a couple of weeks from now, my eldest, about whom we spoke earlier, is back to school. That is, she's heading back to college to begin her sophomore year. I've been making deadlines since she was in third grade; in all that time we've been talking, she and I, about books, about writing, about art and music. She's won a contest for writing a book (in fifth grade!) and she's played keyboard and sung in public (at the county fair) and she's performed at Carnegie Hall (with her high school a cappella group.) For all of those things I have enormous pride. But this fall she's truly busting my buttons, for she's taking a class in Creative Writing.

Yes, I know, you can't push someone into it, nor can you pull. Writing is the thing that causes itself in a person. And I'm not sure I would wish someone into being a writer, because it is difficult, with long moments of extreme dissatisfaction. But I love it so much (that I'm probably doing it wrong), and I want her to have this kind of love for something she does.

And so, I like talk with her about it. About imagery and developing characters. About sitting in public places and taking out your earbuds and really listening to how people speak to each other. I tell her about writers I like because their prose is…elegant, and writers I like because their prose is terse. I talk to her about rules, and breaking rules, and not breaking rules. And sometimes she shows me work, which is the most fun for me, but I cannot let it be so in front of her, because I think the biggest trap for a writer is being satisfied with yourself and having no reason to go on tomorrow.

A lot of these conversations are just politeness on her part. Sitting and listening to me talk. Nodding her head in agreement.

Sure, Dad. Sure, sure. And only a crazy person would wish that she not follow her own roadmap to be someone doing something that has an actual, steady paycheck when she's older. But there are days when I'm a crazy person.

Part of having a daughter who might, maybe, someday, want to be a writer, gives me secret joy. And fear, because writing requires thick skin and fearlessness and a bit of dumbass. Right now, she's none of those. She's sensitive and brave and stubborn. Still, and oddly enough, it's when we're arguing about something and she says, "I didn't say that, I said this," and she goes on to parse her actual sentence. She digs in her heels about the definitions and usage of words.

My God, I love that.

Reading a slap-dash news article: I pop-quiz her. So is it compliance, complacency or complicity? That should be a simple question, right? Or is this my Rime of the Ancient English Major arrogance, rearing its ugly head? We've all seen click-baits where we are treated or subjected to a "look how dumb they are – they got that word wrong," moment. Social media is chock-full of misspellings, poor conjugation, typographical errors, and the occasional, singularly odd made-up word that we can only ascribe to having been originally misheard in a Rolling Stones lyric on AM radio. (Yes, I'm that old...)

And although a selfish part of me wants someone to gripe with about bonehead grammatical mistakes, my daughter's not the one. She's much kindlier than I in that regard. Like her mom, she has a good heart, full of empathy for those folks who say *lesser* when they mean *fewer*. And she doesn't care that it is both flammable and inflammable and rub her hands together slyly imagining there must be a conspiracy theory hidden like an easter egg in there, somewhere.

So when, *when*, is it actually time to fix our actual mistakes? Is there anyone out there who hasn't typed a word then then typed it again accidentally? Do we correct this, or leave it because it's not really important? Did that person mean *sublimely* or *subliminally*? I ask, although I must say that I'm pretty good either way on this one.

What I'm saying is that writing is not solitaire, where you can cheat or screw-up because it doesn't matter, no matter how much it may seem so in the beginning. The goal of writing is to *communicate* with others. Root – commune: to converse or talk together, usually with profound intensity, intimacy, etc.; interchange thoughts or feelings. What I'm most interested in is the concept of profound intensity, and the interchange of thoughts and feelings. Where I come from an interchange is that frightening piece of the highway where other cars are trying to get on or off and must either speed up or slow down to do so. They hesitate, or just wing it – both actions highly risky. Collisions are possible, with no good coming from them. Take care.

Symbolic Logic – November 2018

My younger daughter came home from the first day of school this fall with documents to read and sign. Schools are big on "covenants" and "agreements" between teachers and students and parents – joint pacts to study and teach, to complete syllabi, to not lose or break computers – and so am I. My daughter (the younger) is still in the satisfaction-through-successful-task-completion age and I understand that, too. There are other types of children, of which I was one, who surrender at sixteen to just not delivering the goods. Oh, I learned the stuff, but didn't do the homework, or write the papers or study for the exams and my grades in high school showed that truth. Amply.

I read and signed documents placed in front of me, and she was satisfied and so I was satisfied. We talked about her classes. She was quite pleased with the proportions of friends to classes and the subject matter and the expectations that teachers have of her. She was not so pleased with the number of freshmen on her bus ride home (apparently, they were noisy and insubordinate and had hygiene issues). And what was up with the decision to move away from Macbook to Chromebook laptops? I assured her that they are quite adequate, but she sniffed at my opinion. "So, where is yours?" I asked. "Tomorrow," she said, waving the document I just signed that gives her permission to have one distributed one to her.

Arriving home on the second day of school, she was mightily frustrated. The permission document from the previous day was not the right piece of signed paper. Or it was not sufficiently bureaucratic. Or something. In any case, I had to read and sign a different agreement/contract. And, she explained, they ran out of them in English, so the one she had for me was in Spanish. "You need to sign here, Dad." "Sweetheart? What does the document say?" "I don't know."

Now, I am fully aware of all the triggers this situation had scattered around within it like little gifts in a yard where a big dog lives. The school is short of funding and doesn't want to waste it making copies of documents in English, when they are readily available in Spanish. And I'm a snide, snarky old man with too much time on his hands. And turnabout is fair play, you Anglo-Saxon privileged male. Just sign the damned form.

But here's the thing, thought I. What does this teach my daughter? Does the form have relevant information for me? Is it binding, in some way? Will this come back to bite us? How? Am I not mitigating risk? Is that a good lesson to teach? Can you understand my logic, daughter of mine? Then I need to be able to read the form, before I sign it. At the very least, she needs to be able to read it. My daughter understood this, but still wanted me to sign the form. Is the form unimportant (I asked the bureaucrats in my head)? If so, then give my daughter her laptop and stop wasting time, and when you come across some more forms, send one home. Don't make the unimportant form a hurdle she must jump. My daughter also understood this. But she is practical, and more than another object lesson from me, she needed her laptop. Needed to complete this task (as well as getting on with her homework – trapped inside an application on her laptop). And so, she and I discussed her frustration, (mostly with me for not just signing the damned form) and I was reduced to the point of irritated dad-ness, at which point I failed as a parent. I took the form and wrote "NO" in big letters across the front. Handed it back to her.

Yes, I was wrong. I was wrong, wrong, wrong. But being able to clarify a situation and move on is always the big hammer in my toolbox, and often I'm not permitted to wield it anymore.

The truth is, as I read what I've typed here, I made a rookie mistake, and after fourteen years, shame on me. Because the worst form of *mansplaining* is *dadsplaining*, a word defined as "it's not what you deliver, it's how it's received, dumbass!"

At six-thirty in the evening, there is little one can do about much of anything. You can't call the school. You can no longer make dinner on time. It's too early to go to bed and hope that tomorrow is a better day. In the end you have to suck it up and accept that today you're not as good a stay-at-home-Dad as you've been before. Well…OK then. Shit.

Choice Words – Word Choices – Dec 2018

You may have heard that the statue of the Confederate soldier on the campus of UNC in Chapel Hill was pulled down by protesters, who found it offensive in nature, and whose message of such offense to university authorities was dismissed with, more or less, *get over it*.

You may not have heard that the act of pulling down the statue was criticized by some school authorities as "incomprehensible."

Incomprehensible. Defined as an adjective meaning "unable to be understood."

I to be unbiased politically, but often take grammatical and rhetorical stands, on the behalf of the language. And I must say that I'm not sure what's *incomprehensible* about what happened. Everyone involved in the protest, on any side, was making their point well-known. And those who pulled down the statue did so in front of many other protesters – arguably a fairly strong statement of objection. This was no spur-of-the-moment event, either, so there was a reasonable amount of time for observers to analyze the concerns and feelings of those who wanted the stature removed. Incomprehensible. *Not understandable*. To quote master swordsman Inigo Montoya, speaking to Vizzini the know-it-all, "You keep using that word. I do not think it means what you think it means."

So, was this a malapropism? Did they mean to say something else? Were they zealously and expeditiously trying to respond to the event, and this was the word that availed itself to them? Or was it ironic that the folks in charge were unable to comprehend the offensiveness of the statue's existence, and inadvertently selected that word as a gaslight towards the protesters.

We seem to do that a lot nowadays. Gaslight one another. Talk over each other. When accused of some behavior, we often immediately and hypocritically accuse our accuser of the same behavior. It is a juvenile way of communicating our disagreement or disapproval with things or people.

So, may we suggest some adjectival alternatives? How about "insubordinate?" Insubordinate is defined as "defiant of authority or disobedient to orders." Hey, maybe that's what they actually meant to say in the first place. It makes a little more sense, although the people who pulled down the offending hunk of bronze may not have been students, or perhaps they did not recognize the laws regarding Confederate States of America statues as…valid laws, or maybe they just don't consider themselves "subordinate" to those who would put in place such laws. Some orders, Lieutenant Calley, just shouldn't be followed.

What if they meant incoherent? As in *unclear and confusing*. Nope – everything seemed loud and clear during the protest. Even well-written, from what we saw of posters and signs, on both sides of the protest argument.

Or perhaps they were thinking incompatible. Unfortunately, if something to do with students is incompatible with the university, you may need to re-visit your university's thinking. Because incompatible is defined as "two things so opposed in character as to be incapable of existing together." An epic fail, in a manner of speaking, that would have been true with the statue honoring the Confederacy and its meaning, and many of the people walking past it every day.

Or was it inconsiderate? Yes, and no – because despite common usage, this word actually means *thoughtlessly* causing hurt to others, and this is simply not the case. Much forethought went into their actions – even if it caused hurt. Hurt was a risk involved in the taking down of the icon, admittedly, and yet down it did come.

What about inconceivable? Really? Not if you were remotely paying attention. Not if you know what the word means. Not if you are using it correctly.

The truth, from this desk, and to quote another fine film, is that what we have here is failure to communicate. When someone says "that hurts," we need to believe them and find out what the pain is, and if it can be mitigated, and we are in a capacity to do so, well, do it. If it is hard to relieve the pain, admit it. The word we may be looking for is "inconvenient." Maybe that's what the school meant. What the protesters who pulled down the statue did was *inconvenient.* Defined as *causing trouble, difficulties, or discomfort.*

Yes. That may well be so. Not that this is a real problem, in the end. Because the unspoken message over the years seems to be "get over it." Maybe that's precisely what they were doing. And if you can imagine why this might be so, and if you're smiling, we understand.

Oh my god – I'm that guy! – January 2019

It's January and perhaps now we can finally talk a little about this year's Thanksgiving family get-together meals. But before I get started, I want to let it be known that I miss Turkey (the food – I've never been to the country and cannot actually miss it until I do) and Romaine lettuce, which is acceptably green and crunchy, and pecan pie (I am counting calories and pecan pie really is higher math) and some other things that seem to be troubled by the rules of engagement in our modern food world. Instead, we had chicken, good old reliable and unruffled chicken, with dressing…and it was noteworthy in its adequacy. The cranberry relish, on the other hand, was marvelous, the potatoes good enough for government work and there was wine but I didn't drink any wine, because I don't. Quit judging me. Yes, you were.

There were other things to eat and I ate them, too, but so what? The point of this essay is that the Thanksgiving meal is mostly about talk, and talk we did. Talked about all those things that have stewed in the back of our minds since last Thanksgiving. And, oh boy, there was drama, but now two months later it is no longer as fresh as a new paper cut (with that self-effacing annoyance that it ever even happened because who here hasn't gotten a paper cut and wondered why, oh lord, why me?) So, here's a review:

It may be your opinion that we either caused or exacerbated a problem by spending the whole week together. Actually, it worked very well. Because more of something is always good, right? Can any of you imagine this? Spending a Thanksgiving week together? Madness! Mayhem! And I would like to tell you that we have broken the code on Thanksgiving, but even I cannot lie that baldfacedly. Which may or may not be a word. But here's what I think: I argue with my relatives and friends because I'm supposed to. If you can't talk to those folks, get the toxins out of your system, well, who can you talk to?

Which is my theory as to why it is actually a very good idea that we have Thanksgiving in a rented house at the beach. Because no one has the home-field advantage. You can't escape into your comfort-zone cave, or fetch the car keys and drive off (well, you can, but where are you going to go?)

And I will say right now that this essay seems to be taking a maudlin, basic-cable drama turn, so I'll nip that in the bud right here. What I've actually discovered is something about myself. I miss arguing with my family the rest of the year and I like Thanksgiving. Quite a bit.

Here's the short list of reasons why: my family is pretty smart. I mean, we argue about some important topics, such as how loud do you really need to yell "*bingo!*" when you've filled a row or column in your card? Correct answer – "not that loud, you hurt my ears. And can you take that game downstairs, I want the whole living room to myself and this TV program on how dolphins and some kind of diving bird work together to catch herring." Or: "are you still watching that documentary on baseball? The season is over, move on!" Correct answer – "why don't you carry the garbage down to the curb and hop on into the dumpster, too?" And "who took the last piece of key lime pie? Correct answer - my name is Inigo Montoya and you must die!" With lots of applause for the last one's rhyming scheme, naturally.

We also fuss about politics, religion, science, the bad traffic on the way to the grocery store. The bad traffic on the way home from the grocery store. We do not fuss about there being no coffee. There is always coffee. I mean, we're not animals.

By the way, I am the *paterfamilias*, a role with no authority whatsoever. I can start an argument, but rarely win – even if I'm right, which is a rarity but still statistically possible. I get cranky when they all gang up on me, play devil's advocate, or devil's Uber driver, or devil's sous chef, whichever is necessary to move the ball downfield. But not really cranky. I don't turn up the football game and pout. And it is mostly my fault that we will take an argument to the illogical extreme, or at least what we think is the illogical extreme. Some of you probably throw stuff, or jump up to try and remember the combination to the gun safe. That's not our thing, however – to end Thanksgiving once and for all. Just make it memorable.

In the end, we still *like* each other in my family. All these years later. And there's a new generation of adults, my nieces and nephews, and my own daughters coming up, taking responsibility for leading the discussions. No one is off the hook – escaping from the rest of us trying to be in their business. We talk about each other's problems – the real ones and the ones we just seem to make up out of the evidence we reveal about our lives. For example, my family thinks I'm nuts. I have no idea how this conclusion was reached. Was it my leading another discussion on "mansplaining?" Was it my monthly blog, posted for everyone to see? A rehash of the phone calls I've made to customer service? My home-made bumper-sticker affixed to the wife's car? "Hot Flash! Pull Me Over At Your Own Peril" (This last is pure fiction – but funny, right?)

They expect such behavior from me, and no one takes it particularly seriously. Counselling is suggested, but not mandated. Also, I try to turn the tables on myself before they can, and say "I'm just blustering here, but…" or "pardon my uncredentialled bombast, but…" and they know I'm about as full of shit as I can be full of turkey, which is a lot.

More idle thoughts – February 2019

February. We're in the doldrums of winter (not a real thing) but I'm typing these words back in the shank of the holidays so it could be said that it's really not quite fair to label the whole month like that, however history shows us that February does tend to bite, so, even though I cannot see into the future, an educated guess goes a long way.

On the other hand, seen and pronounced in a particular way, February has the word "brewery" built into it, so you see it cannot be all bad.

I think that the words "doldrums" and "shank" will go the way of the buggy-whip, sooner rather than later. Auto-correct will assist with their demise.

And for what it's worth, even when I'm really in February I'll probably be nowhere near consistently remembering to change to 2019 when I write dates. I'll bet I'm not alone here. Is this because of the dark and cold that our brains don't do this very well? Or do people enjoying summertime in southern Africa and Australia and South America have this same problem? Or has everyone else on the planet already moved to electronic checks and such?

I keep a diary. On paper. In a little book, with an ink pen. I'm such a luddite. Do technically astute people even use that word? What do they call folks who can't program the date on their VCRs? And, oh by the way, when the last VCR dies, some rando Thursday this year or the next, how will we explain technical incompetence in a way that we all understand?

I keep a lot of paperwork in an old leather briefcase. Bic pens, too. And half-read books, just in case. Because when you're stuck somewhere (I don't know – the rest-stop off I-95 outside Santee near the big lakes) and waiting to be rescued (by a tow-truck, or the cavalry, or Parsifal the seeker of the holy grail) you don't want to have nothing to do, or only electronic things to do. You need something that you've already begun – time-tested and reliable. Like a book. One in which you have a pretty good, but not complete, idea of what's going on. Marked with a piece of cardboard.

Batteries suck. Actually.

I keep getting emails for e-harmony. Suggestions. If analytics for data-mining are so advanced, and we're so worried that the big brothers are stealing our private data for nefarious uses, why aren't we all relieved that they have this particular aspect of everything me so very, very wrong? And what is it that we are so worried about, electronic privacy-wise? That we'll get a recommendation that reveals our inner dimwit self? That they'll steal our souls? Personal revelation: I'm not troubled that someone thinks I need to get out of the house and talk to people, have a meal, maybe do some dancing. I probably do.

My wife agrees.

Occasionally, I feel like slugging a programmer in a coffee shop, for their part in the creation of auto-correct. Only my inability to differentiate programmers from soccer moms or gym teachers or goatherders in the coffee shops I frequent keeps this thought-crime from really happening. But, like an astronaut trapped alone on Mars, I'm working the problem, so trust me when I tell you: they're on borrowed time. Insert complex pipe-organ crescendo here.

If I could actually borrow time, I'd like to choose the spring of 1975. There were a few mistakes I made that I would like to have back, like a do-over. When we're teenagers, we tend to think that the world is mostly about us, and that other people – even other teenagers (in fact, particularly them) - are just bit-parts and supporting players in our drama. It's not arrogance, entitlement, electronics or stupidity, though. It's that teenagers' brains aren't fully formed. They're like marshmallows when you put them in the microwave oven, and then press start, and they heat and expand and then explode.

At least that's how it was for me. We could blame electronics, too – they'd just invented Pong and my friend had the game and we all went to his house and played for a whole afternoon. Then we got bored and talked to each other. (Three years later, they invented Asteroids and it used up months of afternoons of my life. I never did learn to do the hustle.)

Anyhow, in my youth I couldn't do the right thing if my life depended on it. And I was slow on the uptake as well. I finally figured some things out…well, last August. So here's my sage advice. Apologize early and often. Edit your work. Ask friends for help. Talk to each other. Read the directions. Eat less and exercise. Smile more. Wash your hands. Put stuff away. Play fair. Don't interrupt.

I have a friend that I like to eat lunch with and have long talks. He is putting off retiring, because he's worried about money. At least that's what he tells me. I'm afraid it's that he is worried about being bored, not having his days planned out for him. I tell him that there is much to do, outside the workplace. Coffee to be drunk. Chess to be played. Walks around the town that need to be strolled. Libraries are full of information that needs to be absorbed. A band somewhere needs a bassist with access to a van.

He says he believes me but is reticent to make the leap of faith. I'm working on him, though. I'll keep you posted.

A Day in the Life – July 2019

Of *course* hot coffee in July. Don't even start with me. This is the definition of dexterity: I can fill the coffee pot with water from the tap without looking at the fill-line on the side of the pot. Eight cups exactly, based on the weight in my hand.

The day begins so early, a rapture of robins and mockingbirds vying for my auditory attention barely after false-dawn. Those moments when daylight wants to peer over its coverlet of clouds but then slips back to sleep. Who can tell the sun what it is supposed to do? I pad downstairs, boot my computer, push yesterday's scrap paper into the recycling bag, strap on my wristwatch, find today's ball-cap. The Mudcats. They're having a rough season. When your pitchers are your parent club's, nothing is certain, nothing reliable. You are a teacher in the third grade, thinking "this child is something, something…," but you will never see the results of that potential, never get to catch that fireball in your own glove.

Take the reader off of its charger. Flip to the most recently achieved page of "Moby Dick." Carry it out to the porch. Wish again that there was a chaise lounge out here, one with the nice cloth cushions that have to be brought in so they don't get mildewed, and best conform to my lumpiness. Go back for the coffee, set the cup on the little table with the citronella lamp – not necessary at this time of day. Cars go by, people heading for the office, to the grocery store for milk or fresh muffins or somesuch. I'm not one of them. I'm reading a book I should have read *in toto* back when I was a shirt-tail lad, but, like so many things, it slipped past me (time and the book) while I was doing other stuff. Now I am of an age where the languorous pace of the prose, the attention to detail, the 'splanation of every little thing to the most absurd length and degree, pleases me greatly. I am in no hurry to finish this yarn (which I know, or think I do, already.) When I finish it, sometime this summer, I will pull another dusty volume off the shelf (1001 Arabian Nights? Jane Eyre? War and Peace? Dubliners?) and plow those fields.

Observation: we hand out reading to youth like punishment. No wonder they don't enjoy it. The world is full of things we do, and things we don't. Reading shouldn't end up one of those things we don't do. Our humanity is in what we think, and how we act based on our thoughts. We are an assembly of event fibers, stretched into threads, spun into skeins of yarns and then woven into the cloth of us. Those yarns are stories, things we've done and said and heard, and read.

My girls are well into their busy days by the time I come back inside looking for food. The kitchen is quiet, except for the click and hiss of the dry cycle of the dishwasher. Anything in the fridge? This and that, poke and hope. Yes, I am no hunter nor gatherer. If it is not fairly readily available, I won't find it, and it won't get eaten. On the other hand, if peanut butter were a wild beast, I would be a tribal elder. I'm not sure exactly what I mean, either.

To the computer, patiently waiting for my password to launch. Do I want to go to the point in the document where I left off last night? How nice of you to ask, inanimate application. Very kind. Now the magic begins – scribbling, editing, layout, art selection, looking at yesterday's baseball scores, reading notes, correcting spelling errors, sipping cold coffee, staring at maps. I'll bet this is how William Faulkner spent his mornings.

I have a small garden growing in the window behind my desk. It is the best place for summer afternoon sun. Succulents, begonias, a coffee-arabica bush in a glazed-clay bowl also containing a small carving of the elephant-headed deity Ganesha. I have read that it is Ganesha who is the bringer of wisdom, good luck and success. Who doesn't want those? But it is also my understanding that Ganesha is lord of obstacles, so that paying him respect may help one overcome…technical difficulties. It seems to me, therefore, that Ganesha is in charge of breaking writer's block. So he gets a place of honor in the shade beneath the lush leaves of my coffee plant.

I am wearing one of those wristwatches that tells me how much I walk and analyzes my sleep-cycles. It is also good for telling the time, I suppose, but who cares? It's a bit strange, somewhat Pavlovian, to have instructions for stopping what you are doing to do something else, even a suggestion so basic as "get up and walk around for 250 steps, please." I am a good student. I save my file, take off my glasses, and walk around the house. Some days I fetch a trash-bag and empty the cans around the house. Yes, yes, I know! Please forward my Nobel prize to the mailing address on the inside cover of this magazine.

At first I didn't like being interrupted when I'm writing. My schedule used to be that I had between 9 PM and midnight to get my work done. Now that the girls are pretty self-sufficient, I have re-captured the daylight hours like MacArthur at Inchon. You know what I mean, with inferior equipment, some problems with the tides and possible loss of the element of surprise.

The neighbor's dogs are barking at the neighbors' dogs. This used to bother me, but now I've become as used to it as I have to the cuckoo clock on the wall (although the half-hourly hooting has been disabled) or the yard-men with leaf-blowers and weed-eaters.

Writer's tip: don't let noise, or the lack thereof, be a reason you can't concentrate on the creative process. I had a roommate in college who stayed up all night and slept in the afternoons. He dipped snuff and left the…expectorant in dixie cups around the room. At first it was the sound of him spitting, every seventy-five seconds or so, that kept me awake at night. I asked him to be more or less regular about it, to no avail. So I just…turned it off. And he stopped making that noise in the room at night. Also, one morning I accidentally tipped over a couple of tobacco spitcups onto his Calculus notes, so that might have had something to do with it. Anyhow, you don't control the world's noise, nor do you really want to poke out your eardrums with your number 2 Berol Black Warrior, so the best thing to do is work through the problem until it isn't one. The same rules apply to social media and checking your email.

Well, I don't have a set list for this concert, but I think I'm about done and I'll bet you could use a break, too. I've been mulling over a sentence that recently formed out of the storm and fog of my mind and offer it up to you as a last bit of advice: life can be either a train wreck or a train robbery, and it's up to you whether or not you're the drunk engineer or the Sundance Kid.

Good luck with that one and *Namaste*.

Rejection – October 2019

My elder daughter told me *you're rambling* the other day, while we were on a drive. Stopped me cold in my verbal tracks. Rambling. What does that even mean? Well, according to the dictionary, "lengthy and confused or inconsequential."

Holy crap. That's bad. Real bad. Lengthy I can live with, but confused or inconsequential? Those are crimes of the first order to a writer.

My first reaction was to be hurt. My god – she basically told me to shut-up. Was she even listening to me? What was I talking about – it had to be something worthy of note. I mean, I'm entertaining, enlightening, filled with as many nuggets of truth as the Klondike River once was with tracer. I can't even remember. Uh-oh. What went wrong? We were in the car, so she wasn't doing homework. Was I interrupting her listening to L'il Naz? My subscription to many-channel radio recently ended, so I was listening to locally broadcast classical music – very quietly because I respect her sensitive ears and despite the lessons of An American In Paris not everyone enjoys waltzes by *Sssssshhhhtrauss*.

And then I started talking. And she asked me, in her inimitable way, to stop. Begging the question: am I tone-deaf to what she wants to talk about, or read, or hear – or was there something else afoot?

No one of us is exempt from the feeling that our ears and eyes are being subjected to unwelcome input. I just googled the word *barrage*, and in addition to "talking too much" the definition of the word included the example of an army firing many cannons over the heads of its soldiers to protect them as they move forward in battle. In addition, a barrage is a kind of dam which raises the level of the reservoir behind it in order to provide water to canals built off the reservoir, for navigation. I'm struggling to see how those go together with "talking too much." Is it a French thing?

Gotta think about this. One word – three apparently unrelated definitions. Or are they?

I'm finished with this summer's beach books – and I have to admit, I like when things…ramble. I enjoy a thousand page read. Am I a dying breed? The truth is I don't get out much, so I have less interaction with others – don't talk enough on the phone, and when I do I like to talk about books and music and politics and current events. I like to talk about what I want. Surely that's normal, right? Doesn't everyone?

Yes, I looked at the sentences I just typed and saw how insensitive they are.

From the moment we wake each morning, we're part of the input of others and they are part of ours. Despite the instagramming of our culture shrinking everything down to infertile kernels and inedible chaff we somehow still communicate with each other. And no matter how much I may choose to feel…rebuffed, am I not guilty of hanging up on cold-callers who…ramble, trying to fit in their sales pitch in one long robo-breath? Don't I flip the thousand-words-in-one bird at the driver who cuts me off in traffic?

And when I'm on the horn with close friends or my sisters – that is, people with whom I share at least same-generation communications skills, do I ramble, oblivious to others yet pleased with the sound of my own voice?

At this point I might say "long story short" but I fear that such a chestnut would turn this into a farce. What my daughter did – and thank goodness – was send me a simple rejection. As a writer I should be used to that, and as an editor, I am reminded that rejections almost always aren't personal. Hopefully, they're part of the process of improvement. With that in mind, I need to be more cognizant of my longwinded speechifying, my off-the-cuff storytelling, my unsolicited soliloquys and rants. I must learn to pull the plug on myself earlier or expect the offstage hoo….

Reader – November 2019

I'm almost certain I've talked about this before – I'm getting older and tending towards repeating myself – but I find that time is getting away from me in ever more slippery-slope chunks. The summer is over here – (and by the time you read this, autumn will nearly be,) and I'm feeling like nothing got done. I mean, by me. Which is a shame, or at least discouraging, so I need to go back and double-check…. You see, I had at least four different books that I planned to consume, and did so. Summer reading is the best – sitting on the front porch as the day's heat dissipates, the buzzing of cicadas and the smell of citronella taking up two of my senses, leaving the others for the cover and spine and open pages in my hand, and the cold beverage on the table next to me. And I have some mighty tomes ahead of me (that, like I said, I will be deep into or will have put paid to by the time you read this).

Reading is not a chore – or it shouldn't be. And assigning myself four books was no challenge. Four doesn't feel like much at all. Not nearly enough. So, what kept me from reading more? I watched baseball, did dishes and laundry, walked, all the normal stuff. I wrote. I always write. Pulled over to the side of the road on the WIP and delved into a different story that had been revving its engines in the corner of my brain. Yes, it got a bit out of control and is now pushing 25K words – which is lunacy, but there you go. I'll get back to the WIP soon. I transplanted some begonia cuttings into flowerpots and kept them alive, for now. I flushed three late guppies and what had been a friendly little catfish from the tank. Human error, in case you're wondering. I'm now staring at the tank, idly thinking about what I might do there next, if anything. I do seem to have a knack for raising healthy algae…. These are not excuses. Well, yes they are. I'm reading more, now. Melville. Twain. Emily Bronte. Emerson. Things I should have attended to long ago.

Over the summer, younger daughter read Mrs. Shelley's Frankenstein as an assignment for her fall English class. I gave her my "Classics Reimagined" copy with all of the brilliant illustrations and other fanciful constructs of this particular volume. It helped her…overcome, if you will, the two-hundred-year-old prose.

She is a good reader, with a hell of a homework-ethic. And by "good" I mean she does what is necessary. She takes her reading assignments and breaks them down into "pages per day," and doesn't deviate from that plan even when something is actually holding her interest. I would say that this is strange and that I don't understand it, but she is seventeen and that describes almost everything about her life right now, from my Dad viewpoint. And the assignments are always completed, so there's that.

But, and this is sort of astonishing, she also reads for fun. She still makes time in her day for something no one told her to do. Perhaps it is precisely because she wants some level of control over her life, for a half hour, forty-five minutes. I know, or at least I hope, that many kids like reading even though they have to do it for some class they're taking. But is this the case, in our world of easy electronic entertainment in the palms of our hands?

Not so long ago (from my perspective, but back when she was in elementary school,) we would journey to the bookstore and she would settle down in the youth/children's section and scan the shelves with discernment, seeking one or two worthy literary candidates. Over the years, she had come to understand that wanting to purchase *everything* came to naught, but if she could show me something she really liked, a volume with a story that stretched her limits, I would consider letting the moths out of my wallet. This happened more often than she will give me credit for.

And, of course, there was always the public library. In her lifetime, it has moved from an old house in our county seat to a new, modern building over by the community college. Once every two weeks or so, we visited there to replenish her stock and return the volumes she'd recently consumed. The adjective *voracious* applied to her. Avid. Bookworm. Bibliophile.

So when I see her with a book, I ask about it. I hear the answer, and nod and say *mmm-hmm*. I may sound non-committal but I am impressed. I never ask her if it's for school, or if it's good, or tell her I'm pleased, because the truth is I'm afraid I'll break it, this phenomenon of reading, like someone thoughtlessly putting a beautiful porcelain tea-cup in the dishwasher.

It is absolutely within the realm of possibility that I am losing it, (and other private thoughts that have escaped from the asylum.) – January 2020

Two bits.

By midwinter I tend to look homeless. Need a shave, a haircut, sunshine. I wear sweaters beneath my jacket, and they hang out. This used to be radically cool – when RAF flyers were the wizards of the air – with long roll-neck sweaters and short wool jackets. And scarves. Goggles. OK – belay the goggles, but cool hats, tipped jauntily. And they were twenty-two or -three years old, so, there's that. I am nowhere near twenty-three anymore, and tip well past the maximum weight for a Supermarine Spitfire. (Still, I have dreams I am in a kite over Herefordshire or Hampshire arm-wrestling Dorniers or some such. This is all a synaptic manufacture of my still childish dreams, but I wake up feeling like a Player and a cup of tea. I hope this never goes away, is what I'm saying.) Having wandered away from my point, and only just now returned, my family is generally appalled by my appearance. I would say that I'm sorry and I hope to do better, but that would be a lie and I'm averse to such fibs. I like winter for its acceptance to some extent of raggedy, slovenly appearance. Don't we each of us own some old mittens well past their prime, or a toboggan from school days? Put them on. Stick out your tongue at those who would look down their noses. Don't lick the flagpole, tho…

We Wish You a Hairy Catfit (what the recent holidays have become.)

My sister asked if she could bring the pies. Four of them. "No one else should make pies" she said. When I asked why not, she said "I have it under control." Oh, OK. But my argument: you just cannot have too many pies. No one is going to judge you for any reason I am aware of if you have three apple pies and two pecan and a couple of pumpkin. Chocolate chess. Oh, and mincemeat. Even if someone says they don't even like mincemeat pie, you can have one on the card table, ready to be served. Why? Because this is America, dammit. Or something like that. An inalienable right, like voting, singing in the shower, and/or picking your nose in private. Yeah, and that speech thing. The right to tell someone who doesn't like mincemeat pie that they are welcome to shove a slice of it.... Just kidding.

Woof.

One daughter of mine wants a cat. The other recently got a dog for a few weeks and discovered that being a student in a one-bedroom apartment with a full class schedule and work-study don't mix. She was very sad when she gave it to a friend to care for it, but she now understands what I've been saying for a little while. I know, many folks make keeping pets work. Some don't. It's not one more thing that divides our nation, just an individual decision each of us makes. The person who owned our house before us had a cat. It shed. We know this because the refrigerator broke about a month after we moved in and the repair-person found a substantial amount of feline-dander in the fridge's guts when it was turned around. The condenser took the worst of it, I think. We might have created a whole new kitten if we'd been given some time and a bit of magic.

By the way – I don't mean to say that some people actually make their pets *work*. Well, some do, of course, like herding sheep or ferreting out illicit drugs or guarding piles of baseballs hit over the fence by little boys, but not cats. I mean, you're killin' me, Smalls - cats don't work. Not for love nor money. I mean, cats are most effective at being feline, but you cannot make a cat do a blessed thing on command. You know what I'm trying to say, don't you? Certainly you do.

Pranks. Thanks.

On a completely different note, I recently bought a small aerosol can of "new car smell" at the Ace hardware store. It cracks me up a little bit to spray it in the can after…dropping a load. And so much better than anything floral – which instead of disguising the abominable event, instead presents a whole new olfactory horror, like giant, ancestral hummingbird's fossilized doody. I do not, however, recommend duplicating this prank at home. I have spent my entire adult life doing such…irresponsible and yet (for the most part) harmless things and while it is not "expected" it is "comprehended" that I know I've done something wrong and am not particularly penitent.

Praise be…

Never let it be said that I left a terrible idea on the table. Or let it be said, it's all the same to me. It turns out I just might be that guy who goes one step too far, every time. Or tells the Dad joke that mustn't be spoken aloud. Pull my finger. That said, here is another possibility: using that new car smell under my arms as deodorant, just before going to church service. Dear God, what is that odor? It smells like -- *victory*….

Call Me Triceratops.

And speaking of fossilized, I am glad to hear that my own name is one of those boy's names going "extinct," according to a recent clickbait passing for news. That is, the diminutive version of my given name was assigned to very few newborns last year and is expected to be applied to even fewer this year. Good riddance. It isn't a very fine name, sorry Mom and Dad, and is frequently a joke name for characters in Hollywood film and television scripts. A kind of bonehead name – doofy and not very bright. A name should have gravitas, and yet be short and sweet if necessary. A boy's name needs to be…manly and yet playful. Or is that very old school? Am I falling into the binary ditch, the patriarchal nonsense of a bygone age? I don't know. Once upon a time, very much *ago*, a quite famous actor wielding the appellation made it beloved and taken seriously. Heroic, even. But the numbers of kids with my name continue to shrink, so, read into that whatever you will.

Personal – March 2020

A couple of things. I've noticed that my oldest daughter has become something of a conscience for me. She is aware that I have a checkered past of mansplaining, being rather knee-jerk judgmental, and never quite current with social trends. She, on the other hand, is young and also tough and erudite and forgiving and verbose, and her arguments spill out of her filled with logic and heart and plenty of new information that has not necessarily crossed my radar. She doesn't shrink from engaging with me both barrels blazing. She is a teacher. And I welcome that.

We recently discussed (actually I asked her to clarify) the proper use of personal pronouns in conversation, and how folks (particularly in social media) present theirs in much the same way we used to hand over business cards back in the '80s. And lest that remark be seen as semi-snarky and become hardened like enamel to my already sketchy reputation, I did at the time already understand why in a society that is no longer thoughtlessly binary we should and do pay attention to how we are referred and how we communicate with others. Identity is important and relevant. And having a part of that very identity missed or dismissed in conversations between us can be just as damaging and hurtful as actively saying something mean.

And I might have used the adverb "unintentionally," rather than actively, but it's not really that way at all, is it? Because the first definition I find for that particular word is "not done on purpose," which is a vague and idiomatic phrase we can hide behind if we must. What does "on purpose" mean, anyhow? Does it mean "with purpose?" Or is it more closely aligned with "I wasn't thinking of that result when I did that?" Or, perhaps, it is "I wasn't thinking at all of the possible results when I did that?"

Because one of the bits I've picked up on in social media is the rash of passive-aggressive commentary.

And while we're here, I am tired of the term "my bad," which sounds intentionally childish and petulant, and not at all like an apology. In my opinion, it shouldn't be accepted as one.

Anyhow, what I have concluded in my conversations with my daughter is that we are often creatures of mere habit, or more accurately, people, comfortable or not, in our own personal ruts. We tend to do what we are used to doing, say what is most often said by or to us. We think, behave, respond as if we haven't learned a thing since we were twelve. All of the dumb in us is coagulated in our pipes and doesn't permit anything fresh inside.

The reason I bring it up at all, is because I am curious. Is it possible, I posed to my daughter, that our conversational habits and norms are the problem, and not just the grammatical and social exactitude of personal pronouns? I mean, probably it's not the front burner problem with humanity, but is it part of it?

You see, I think that when we speak to each other, we just don't listen enough. We don't speak enough in the second person. That is, we don't say "you" enough. How are you? What are you up to? How's your day been? It tends to be more of "what is up with her?" and "Why is he like that?" Perhaps we have a proclivity for gossip. Or we've become defensive about ourselves. Afraid that we will be judged.

I had a friend a while back who might have been the best salesperson ever. Always asked for the order. Consistently made her sales numbers.

But it wasn't just her sales patter, nor her product knowledge, or even magic beans which made her a success. What she brought to the table was that she was a natural *listener*, someone who looked at you while you were talking, smiled, attended to your words, nodded when she liked or agreed with something you said. When you took a breath, she would repeat some of what you had just said back to you, as in "I think that what you say about conversations makes sense, Garry. Why do you think that is?" And that leading question she posed – the *why* question (which I often claim to not know what to do with) - would nudge the conversation forward, gently and in a way that made you feel...worthy of talking and being talked with. It demonstrated her interest, and that what you had to say was genuine, no matter the topic. And the icing on the cake for both of you was that she asked and learned about you. She knew what you were doing, how it was going, what was coming next for you. As a customer, you felt necessary and your needs understood. As a co-worker, you felt a real partnership. I may be oversimplifying, but this way of conversing made her good at creating friends from strangers and customers and colleagues. And in my opinion, we're just not very good at this anymore.

I don't have all the answers. I'm just suggesting that it might be time to listen, to ask leading questions, and to be interested in the person with whom you're talking, and not just some of the words coming out of their mouth. Even, occasionally, ask why. Put down the phone, turn off the TV, shift in your chair so you are facing one another. Get the conversation rolling, and if it slides into a rut in which you find yourself talking/judging/gossiping about a third person – he, she, they – bring it back to *you*. That is, don't let the conversation drift into the weeds, return to the person at whom you are looking, their face, the subject at hand.

April – April 2020

Recently, that is in the past five years or so, I've begun to notice that I "define" and "judge" with the same fat paintbrush. I'm not proud of it, but there you are. Just another opinionated older man with some sort of chip on his shoulder.

So what exactly do I mean about defining and judging? That in the act of believing that my input is needed on a subject, I am simultaneously deciding something about my audience. And as I think I'm clearing the air, I become part of the reason it…smells.

It's not too late, though, is it? I can cure myself of this malady. Not completely by myself, of course. I have very good people who want me to not end up a curmudgeonly old bastard who no one wants to be around. So then how do I fix this rut I've driven myself into. Introspection might help. A bit of my daughters looking over my shoulder while I type might also be useful.

What are the circumstances where I find myself in that mode, frustrating and in disagreement with others? Where do I socialize? Where do I get in trouble?

I ask that because the only social media platform I still use is Twitter and it is a bit ironic that nothing about it is faintly birdlike. Admittedly, my presence there is a bit silly: I haven't many followers, and myself follow mostly local folks and other writers and editors.

Wait – did I just use the word "silly" to explain my feelings about Twitter? That sounds like judgment to me, too. Backspace/erase. What I meant to say is one could find my use of Twitter more on the order of observer than active participant. Indeed, I sometimes begin a tweet, or a response to someone else's, and then stop in mid-thought, suddenly aware that I have nothing useful to add to the mix. Delete my thought. Leave the virtual premises. Find something useful to do.

Still...

I see writers post on Twitter their hopes and fears about WIPs, the process of writing, the search for the right words, crowd-sourcing names for characters, places and titles and telling how they feel about submitting and getting rejected or accepted. In my judgment (uh-oh), they seem to be frustrated or elated with equal abandon. They love and hate editors and publishers. Do I understand this? You bet. It's a real bitch working in a vacuum, with only some vague idea what will happen at the end of each step. Their confidence in themselves, their writing groups, their agents, and the opinions of their loved ones seem to be one day of writer's block away from being dashed, and social media seems like a monkey-rope to like-minded individuals going through the same crap. I mean, it sucks being a writer.

On the other hand...

Editors tend to post all business-like, about reading schedules and press releases and they like to announce what's up in the next issue and then they descend all *my precious* into how so many authors are difficult or easy to deal with (in the submission stage) and how deep or insurmountable the slush pile is and what in the world is this hack thinking who bites the hand that feeds them or can't follow basic submission guidelines? And such post-threads are can't-look-away fun to read and tricky for me to stay out of the mosh pit. Yes, yes, all writers are self-centered layabouts with no idea what it takes to run a railroad.

It totally sucks being an editor, too.

There seems to me to be a general mood (is there such thing as an anecdotal mood?) among the writing/editing/publishing, selling and reading *community* that we're at odds with one another. That writers compete for readers, that bookstores are fighting each other for the same disposable income, and that editors can't decide on a unified theory for Oxford commas. I've seen authors post the idea that they should be compensated financially for their efforts. Yes, say I. If one can get recompense for a story, essay or poem, then that is a good thing. And no good comes from having an online debate with writers and editors about supply-side economics in the *community*. Come on, I suspect that every editor would prefer to be a paying enterprise. And yet no editor should be berated for not being able to be one. If a publishing team has found a way to produce a literary organ but is not quite able to make a profit from it, then it is still a good effort, worthwhile and valuable to the *community*. Submit to it, if you want. Don't if you don't.

On the other hand, editors should not take it personally when the occasional writer goes a bit rogue on them in social media or even in a response to a response email. If someone asks if you're a paying market, answer the question. If they ask *why not?* well, answer the question. If it's a trigger-question, let it go. Let it go. I'm against blackballing, giving a writer a piece of my mind (I haven't much to spare, honestly), or ghosting. I've had a contributor apologize to me for not getting back to me before I've already accepted their submission to let me know that they were accepted somewhere else. And I suspect that the timing was close, and possibly the other venue was a paying gig. Well, good for them for being paid for their efforts, and as for me, I congratulate them and then shut up and go back to work.

In the end, I hope I'm learning something. If I've nothing useful to add, or even if I think I might, move on. That's my "over the shoulder" crew's unit of measure. A friend recently gave me a jar of "umami dust," for giving distinctive flavor to soups, roasts, stews. You know umami? The Cambridge English dictionary online defines it as "a fifth taste, sort of like savory, only not." Just kidding. They really tried, I'm sure, but it's not useful to just tell us it has something to do with glutamates, when we don't even know what glutamates are, other than sounding like the team name for the University of Southern New Hampshire.

I want to be the textual equivalent of umami dust. Somehow, I will try to get there, without driving everyone else nuts.

Prayer – May 2020

Difficult times. I don't need to tell you that, but I want you to be aware that I am aware. What is there to say that hasn't already been said, or that troubles that which is already disturbed? Good question….

My thoughts are divided into four unequal quadrants: What I know, what I think, what I believe and what I don't know. What I know consists of those things I can verify as facts. What I think consists of those things I have some knowledge of, but cannot prove or verify. What I don't know is that very large set of things about which I yet have shown no interest in or may yet encounter and develop that interest. It is also all things I have tried to learn but cannot. And what I believe is that which I have only hope or faith in but cannot verify or prove. I choose to call the divisions between these thoughts *quadrants*, but this may be a misnomer as there is certainly overlap, for example, between what I know and what I don't know and what I think and what I don't know.

To give you an example of what I'll call quadrant 1, I know that when I type this document and use my software application's save function, I can put an electronic copy of it into a file on my computer's hard drive. It is knowledge that I have had for quite some time, and yet it is new knowledge that did not exist for anyone on earth before I was born, in fact, barely before I became an adult. Computers have not had such capabilities for very long, in the scheme of human existence.

It may be argued by some that I do not know that the computer behaves like this, because sometimes computers make mistakes. The argument is that I only *trust* that the electrons do what I tell them to. What this is, unfortunately, is a failure in the knowledge of some people. They cannot see, or do choose to agree that particle physics does what it does. I cannot see it, either. It can also be said that I don't know the math that makes particles do what they do, so I don't actually *know* what I think I know.

Hmmm.

What often happens in a discussion like this is the argument, that is the discussion using reason, not the idiom for fighting with words, deteriorates into something ad hominem, which is a point of fallacy or something anecdotal which may or may not be evidence but by itself isn't scientific. It is insufficient, a term that implies and should be inferred as only my opinion, to say "let's agree to disagree." Indeed, I am troubled that I hear this so often. There must be some way to have truth and facts, without everyone squaring off in corners, gloves down. Let's just say that What I Know has the least solid foundation of the four quadrants. As well it should.

To continue…

What I think is a rather large quadrant. That's because I think a lot, about lots of different things. People, my friends and family. Places I've been and want to go, and history and music. Poetry takes a lot of my thinking, and wordplay in general. I think, like many writers do, about my work-in-progress, what is coming together and what's still broken, and what needs to still be figured out. I don't have much free time, because I'm not sure precisely what that means to most people, but I try to keep a lot of balls in the air, am rarely bored, and don't consider thinking as wasting time or "doing nothing." What I think has been full of things like "I think she likes me" and "I think that the first Star Wars is the best," as well as "planets are spherical because gravity makes them be that way," and "coffee is better than tea." As you can see, this is largely opinion, only some of which is based on anything remotely resembling empirical evidence. All of it is arguable, particularly that first one. Sometimes, however, the Think quadrant has good information. "I think that it is difficult for someone to make a living as a poet" skirts that fine line between the Knowledge and the Think quadrants, with even a couple of toes in the "I don't know" quadrant.

I'm not going to spend a lot of time on the What I Don't Know space. It is infinite, of course, and ever growing, if that is even possible. I don't know much about astrophysics, and I don't know anything at all about TikTok. And so on, and so on. I don't shy away from my lack, however. I embrace it. Not in the way that sounds, however, like I'm happy in my ignorance. I embrace that there is an infinite variety of things to contemplate and discover, and I reach out into that set to find new interests. I hope to do this as long as I am able.

What I believe. And now, the tricky one. We are so inclined to interchange the words "I believe" with "I think" that it becomes hazy what we really mean. Do we really believe that this Sunday we switch back to Daylight Savings? Do we really believe that it's going to rain this weekend, or that there's another jar of mayonnaise in the pantry? We say things like this all of the time. And it turns our communications with one another just one more notch to the difficult. I know what I believe. I know that what I believe cannot be proven – that it is based on the concept of faith, which is a different collection of knowledge and thinking on my part (hence some more overlaps in my quadrants.) But I try to never confuse it with things that I think can be proven (yes, there is more mayo), and I am not troubled by the idea that details underlying beliefs are sometimes questioned by those who need more evidence, or proof. Or pose questions to me about what can or cannot be done.

That's a good start, I think. I don't know. I know I'll come back to this. I believe it has potential for being useful. Like I believe that things will get better. I think it will take time. I know that we've been through difficult times before and come through them. I don't know how it will look at the end.

And I hope you are OK.

Memory – June 2020

By now this should come as a surprise to no one, but when I was a *shirt-tail lad* as my grandpa used to call me, I wasn't the best-behaved child. Case in point, one Friday evening my dad was relaxing in his chair, reading the paper, when he was informed that he had to drive Mom to a meeting at church, so all of us had to pile into the VW bus we owned – our only car. My sisters and I were already in pajamas, on the floor in the gray glow of the TV before bedtime. *Let's go*, he said. *But Dad, we're watching!* I groaned generously on behalf of the children in the family. Let's go, he repeated quietly, his single prescribed unit of patience expended. My sisters extended me silent, single shakes of their heads, and got up from their spots, so naturally I thought it best to repeat *But Daaaaadd...!* with more emphasis. *Now*, he barked – the Dad trump-card which warned off any future argument by sane individuals. *Aww, Dad*, I said anyway, because getting the last word when you're not getting your way is an ancient debate tactic and also because I do not reside in the quartile marked "sane individuals with a good bead on reading someone's mood" on any quadrant-chart. I got the not one more word Dad-glare I deserved. *Wear your slippers*, my mom said helpfully as we herded outside.

The ride to church, about two miles from home, was as uneventful as one could expect with antsy children in a car, and a shot-gun-sitting mom's hand free to freely swat in response to signs of unruliness. We dropped her off, with the plan that she would catch a ride home with one of her church-friends and off we put-putted, Dad lighting up a Raleigh and my sisters and I, at first quietly and then not so, playing grab-ass, pinching, generally pestering each other in the back seats, then stopping and sitting with hands folded in the hopes that no one or the other of us would draw his righteous ire. Which rhymes with fire. Then, with no evidence that our behavior had been noticed by him, we naturally started up again; slowly, cautiously, then with gusto until my little sister stage-whispered that she was receiving all of the pinches. In such ways do siblings establish, maintain and evaluate pecking order. My older sister hissed at us to stop, and then pinched me, of course.

Dad took a different route home from church, one that would first go through downtown before following the long, twisting suburban avenue that would place us back in our driveway. Perhaps he was bored. Perhaps he was thinking of picking up something from the drugstore. Perhaps he enjoyed the drive, watching the sun set, now that he was out here. He let the cigarette prop in the corner of his mouth, and I sniffed the smoke as it wafted into the back of the VW. There was no car-radio (for either entertainment or covering noise in our old car,) because that would have cost extra, so only the sound of Dad pressing the clutch in and smoothly shifting gears and the whooshing breeze in his open window venting out the smoke covered our backseat foolishness. It was just a matter of time. Mere moments, actually. Because it had been so satisfying to pinch her before, I gave my little sister another. It was just a peep of a whine, like the distant yowl of a kitten having its tiny tail stepped on by an old woman going to the kitchen in her cottage to pour herself another cup of chamomile tea.

That's it! Dad growled, kicking the clutch and brake together and bringing our microbus to a gravel-skidding halt on the side of the road. *I've had it!* He leaned over the back of his seat and pointed at me. *Alright, mister! You just earned yourself a walk home!*

Dad always said things like that. Nevertheless, it required my still rather undeveloped brain a few moments to understand what he meant. Oh. Get out of the car. *But I'm wearing my pajamas*, I whimpered, more concerned about that than where were we? and did I know how to get home from here? and how far was it? and my dad is kicking me out of the car! and the other jumbled thoughts rattling around in my skull. My sisters didn't even look at me, instead staring straight ahead like Midwest housewives as if the VW was still in motion and hadn't yet reached their stop. This may very well have been the etymological root of the term "throw him under the bus." I pulled the handle down and got out, closing the car door behind me. OK, let me back in, I thought. I've learned my lesson. Nope. With a German-engineered mechanical raspberry, the VW pulled away and there I was, standing in the gutter in my slippers and flannel jammies.

Crap. Crappity-crap.

It is a well-known social phenomenon that we all have dreams about being somewhere we don't want to be in a mode we wouldn't choose. At school, standing in front of the class doing a difficult math equation on the board in only our underpants. Why? Because math is hard and because, as I've said before, *underpants* is the funniest word in the English language. Being forced to do math up at the blackboard and caught wearing only underpants is, by proxy, the most embarrassing combination our subconscious can dish up. However, I suspect that having actually acted out such a thing – standing on the side of the road in my hometown in my pajamas trying to figure out how to get home without being seen – my subconscious no longer finds it sufficiently cruel and unusual. It now prepares scenarios for me that would curdle milk, peel the siding off the house, send a normal person screaming into the night.

Moreover, let it be known my fight-or-flight instinct contains almost no measure whatsoever of "fight" and a double-big-boy helping of "flight." Spinning slowly in a circle, I got my bearings and lit out for home. Running along the sidewalk in the gloom of sunset, past the stinking blue-green catch-pond at the chemical plant, past the bank and train-station, through town just before streetlight sensors turn them automagically on while pharmacies and hardware stores wrap up the day's business with one more customer pulling up in front to fetch a bottle of Bayer aspirin, a ball-peen hammer, or grabbing a Hallmark card for an nearly-forgotten wedding anniversary. Hey! See the nine-year-old boy in his pajamas scamper past with a look of terror on his face? Strike you as odd?

I might have made it all the way home, I don't know…let's call it *unscathed*…, but about halfway there one of the moms from my neighborhood was Oldsmobiling back from a get out of the house for a moment trip to the supermarket and saw me chugging along and pulled over, rolling down her car window and shouting my name. *Is everything OK? What are you doing out at this time of night? Are those your pajamas? Do you need a ride?* Fortunately, by the time I was nine I had already learned that choosing to politely answer only one of multiple questions would be seen as performing the job of communicating with adults to sufficiency.

Why, yes, I said, panting. *Yes, thank you, I could use a ride.*

Now, it needs to be said that at this moment my Dad had completed going around the block and returned to the place where only minutes earlier he'd most ceremoniously dumped me like a cat he no longer wanted to have as a pet. My sisters had already said the unnecessary and yet magic words, "Dad, he's gone." Dad had leaned out and shouted my name in much the same way my neighbor had. God in heaven must have chuckled a little at the synchronicity.

He drove down the street I had just moments earlier run along, turned around (rather than heading home and possibly seeing me scurrying along the side of the street) and retraced his path, scoping left and right for what he thought he would see - a pajama'd, crying child. Turned and tried again. Thumped the steering wheel with his fist. Shook his head when my big sister said, "Oh, no. You've lost him," and my little sister began to cry. Dad turned one more time and headed back to church to get Mom.

Dropped off by my bewildered neighbor (whose private theories about our family were now supported by ample evidence), home and alone, I scurried upstairs to my room, kicked off my slippers and climbed under the covers. I knew I was in deep trouble – abyssal - would have…heck to pay later, and wanted one last night of peace to rest up for whatever was coming my way.

And that was the end of the story, from my certain perspective.

But let it be said, let it be written, that the following day, as I always did on Saturday mornings, I went out to play. Shooting baskets at my friend's house that morning, his mom came out and asked *so what happened last night?* which is out-of-the-blue-parent-speak for I know you did something and I want the details, sporto. I swear I thought she was talking to her son, but she kept looking at me and he was now looking at me (with some relief, I might add that whatever it was that he had done, she wasn't asking him about it, yet) and if I had had a mirror at that moment, I would have looked at me. And because nothing particularly special had happened that I wanted to talk about, I shrugged. *I mean,* my friend's mom asked, *why were the police driving around with bullhorns calling your name?*

What?

And so, it turned out that Dad and my sisters had picked up Mom, somehow explained what he'd done while all of them together drove around looking for a child crying in his pajamas by the side of the road somewhere, then gave up and went to the police station to report what had happened. And the police gave him the stink-eye and then set out to find me, in the gloom of a Friday evening. Cruising the suburban streets of town, shouting my name through bullhorns.

Yeah. That can't have gone well. I guess I'm glad I wasn't there, or found immediately or even soon. And when I was discovered, later, in bed asleep, (because my parents went upstairs to find a piece of laundry of mine for search dogs to sniff) – oh, hell, yes – it was a kind of miracle that they chose to not wake me up and, I don't know, *strangle* me in front of the cops.

Another Day In The Life – July 2020

Mom's OK. She has a one-bedroom apartment in her stepped-care facility, the Home, and feels pretty good. She's lost some weight during the pandemic lockdown, not because there's no food, but because she's paying attention to it, not nibbling snacks so much, not getting dessert at both lunch and dinner.

Here's how it goes. Wake up and putter around until she wants some coffee or tea, and get that made. Turn on the music channel she likes on her television. She likes the popular classical station. Lots of Mozart and Ravel and Chopin and Tchaikovsky. Less Mahler. When she wants to listen to Mahler, she pulls out a CD from Pop's old collection and puts it in her boom-box. That thing needs replacing – the volume control does volume but has little control. It was only about thirty bucks, so it's done what was expected of it, but as soon as her place allows visitors again, I'll fetch her a new one. I would send it to her, but she cannot read the set-up instructions, so it will have to do for now. With her coffee (or tea) she may sit and look at the puzzle or crossword for a while, if it's a sunny day. If not, maybe put such things away until tomorrow. She might read, instead. Large print books, from the nice library that they have at the Home. Or ones we've sent her. She finished Towles' A Gentleman In Moscow and is wrapping up Educated by Tara Westover. We just mailed her American Dirt. I hope she likes it as much as we did. When she's done, she'll give them to the library for others to read. That's how it should always be with books, right?

Time for breakfast. She gets some of her groceries from delivery from the store, and extra milk from the cafeteria for cereal. When she's done she takes her meds. Blood pressure and cholesterol stuff. She manages her Type II diabetes well. She took a tumble back during the fall, a stumble in the hallway. Was in a wheelchair for about two months. Went to PT to get her legs back in shape afterwards. Now she has some days where her legs don't want to behave exactly how she wants, and she uses a walker. Other days, she can navigate around the Home – going to the clinic to have her temperature checked, or the library with her mask on, or out to the garden where there are some benches so she can sit in the shade and feel the June breeze.

There are some friends who do this, too. There's no plan for it – sunny days they just end up at the benches, masked and with enough distance between them. There's one woman who talks too quietly behind her mask, and they have to tease her to speak up so that they can hear her over the sparrows in the trees. Mom says that the little raised vegetable garden she can see from her patio, started a couple of years ago by local college students and a bit run down and overgrown now, has some volunteer tomatoes and arugula. There are also a few fig trees around the campus that they can grab ripe fruit from, if they beat the grackles and cardinals to them. Ooh, I don't like figs, one of her friends says. Mom smiles beneath her mask and says nothing. Figs are awesome and go well with toast and peanut butter.

Or, if it's raining, she sits next to the sliding glass door that leads out to the patio and listens to it falling on the trees and pavement. Lunch is delivered at the previous day's dinnertime, so she's got it out of the fridge and nukes it for a moment. She's told me she doesn't like the chaise longue she bought herself a year ago because it takes up too much room, but that's where she relaxes, eats her salad and sandwich, listens to her music. We ordered her canned soup – lots of different varieties, but it was on back-order for so long that it seemed better to hang onto it until the weather gets cool again.

The phone rings, and it takes four to get to it. We check in with her every day or so. My older sister calls every single day, and they talk for an hour. Here's what's going on here. How are you doing? Do you need anything? My brother in-law calls from work to tell her a joke every day. We sent her some sugar-free lemon drops a month ago. For some reason the best deal was twelve bags of them, so now she has about 9 pounds of lemon drops. Yes, that's loony and yes, we talked her out of putting some of them out in the common area to share, which would be what happened in any other time in her life.

There is a friend in the Home she calls The Cookie Lady who every day for twenty years baked a batch of cookies and went from cottage to apartment to room giving her cookies to her friends. That was how she spent her days. Can you imagine always having the perfume of newly baked cookies about you? She's 102 now and has a twenty-four-hour caregiver and cannot bake cookies anymore. Mom calls her on the phone and if The Cookie Lady is having a good, lucid day they talk, and they also talk if she's not.

Mom prefers to do some things in the afternoon. Wash clothes. The washers and driers are down the hall, and usually empty this time of day. If you call her during this time, you may get her voicemail and have to call back in a little bit. Her walker holds the laundry basket just fine. It takes a little time to get down there, set up the loads, get them done, dried and folded. Walking back and forth is good exercise. Then supper arrives from one of the masked and gloved caregivers. She knows everyone by name, and they know her. Afterwards, she cleans up the kitchen, and winds down for bed.

She watches a little news in the evening, then switches back to her music. Too much news is not just overwhelming, but it is also a bummer. If it's not too late, and we haven't talked today, it's a good time to call. We always say I love you and I'll talk to you soon. We laugh together about how her always telling us as kids to wash our hands has done us well during these complicated times.

Decompression – August 2020

I have recently completed writing a first draft of a new novel. I understand that some choose to celebrate when they reach this milestone, like a marathon runner finding the last bit of energy to raise their hands to cross the finish line, waving a banner or spilling a little champagne around, but that's not what I did. Before I wrote, in those heady days of nine-to-five, I imagined that this was a time for scotch and a cigar or something like that, but perhaps I've gotten old (and more aware of the time left to me, an unknown quantity but still something definable – a small handful of decades at best. So I typed those magic words – The End – and filed the opus away in three or four real and virtual spaces so that hopefully it won't get wiped or lost. I will get back to it, to rewrite and edit as necessary.

If this sounds like a textbook definition of underwhelming, I suppose it was. Where was the party? What was the reward for a difficult task well done? And where were the many people – family and friends – who supported me in my work? Where are my sycophants, my groupies, the people fawning over each word I speak and waiting with hidden recorders for those words I haven't yet applied to paper? Hoping to capture a bon mot or catch me in a truth. Or a lie.

There aren't any fireworks or parades. And for this I am thankful. Because I am not very good at that part of writing-that-has-little-to-do-with-writing. I'm not the marketing guy, the social butterfly, the tall one at the cocktail party smiling and laughing and witty about any subject. I'm not an analyst or a critic or a hanger-on. And I'm more-or-less unpublished. Oh, I know about the writer's platform, and about submissions and cover letters and everything else that goes with it. I'm just not with it.

I prefer to get back to work. That's not practical, however, when one has been deep in a WIP. I think that to jump into something else, something new, without…decompression can give a scribbler the bends. The storytelling bends, with bubbles of the previous story relentlessly working their way into the new yarn, precisely where they don't belong.

Instead I've been pacing around the house for a couple of days, revving the engines, sitting down to the computer and immediately standing up again. I pull books off my shelves, looking for something to make my mind slow down or speed up, go someplace other than the last pages of the story I just finished. It is far too early in the process of writing/editing to begin second-guessing my work, wincing at the things I thought were funny, shaking my head at those bits that I imagined profound. I do, however, take notes, put them on an app in my phone and file them by date.

Here's one: "There's no place in the scripture where it says that Grace is immediate. It makes more sense that it comes with a grace period."

I have no earthly idea where that peculiar gem fits in my novel, but it's in my notes, so there you are. Another entry says just the two words "tantalizing stench." Yep. I like it, but that's a head-scratcher, too.

I'll eventually edit. In the meantime, the story needs to air out, like crushed grapes fermenting in the barrel. Then I can see it from the right distance and should be able to do the rewrite justice.

I tell myself that I require little to no acknowledgement for my writing. That said, it is just as plausible that I deserve little to no…success. What I mean, of course, is that this – the norms of authorship - are not why I write. But why I do write is not easily explained. I have stories. I like telling them. I think they are good stories, and I am able to tell them well. Maybe I'm wrong. So did I lie in the previous paragraphs? Do I really want no kudos? The truth is I don't know.

At this particular place in my life – the downstairs "office" I've commandeered out of the dining room – I just like typing my words into the computer, a cup of cold coffee at hand, the radio on the classical station so quiet I can barely hear the brassy blare of Tchaikovsky, much less the softly blowing leaves of Liszt. It's a good workspace. There's a comfortable chair in one corner, I highly recommend it for taking a nap.

There are books on the shelf next to it. I'm trying to read things I never read before but should have. And, because we live in stranger than before times, there's also a five-pound bag of Idaho baking-spuds. My office has become an extension of our pantry. It's excellent that there's a mini-fridge near my desk, but not a drop of beer resides within. Butter. An extra dozen eggs. Leftover tomato-sauce from last night's spaghetti dinner.

I don't mind the intrusion of noise - I'm not living in a cloister – there's traffic to the kitchen next door all of the time. The scent of grilled-cheese sandwiches. The cacophony of the blender making a smoothie. My daughters will both be off to school soon, and I relish their being here right now and will miss the chaos of them when they are out. I smile when they say, "what are you up to, Dad?" They know perfectly well, of course.

I like telling a story – good, bad or indifferent. I have fun reading them aloud; to others, yes, but just as satisfyingly to myself. My wife comes down from her own office and asks me who I'm talking to. Myself. Oh, OK, she says and grabs a bowl of cereal and retreats back upstairs. I appreciate that level of comprehension, of appreciation.

And so, as the man says, it goes. I type, I read, I think, I pace in proscribed circles. I look out the window, to see if the sun is past the yardarm, so I can go and sit on the porch for a while. It's a writer's life.

We Got the Beat – October 2020

Sixty-three years ago, September fifth as it turns out, Jack Kerouac's "spontaneous prose" novel was published. His girlfriend at the time wrote about that moment when they read the first reviews of the book - disappointing and yet insightful criticism of something the established literary world didn't yet understand. The girlfriend - Joyce Johnson - said that Kerouac had that last night of obscurity and the next morning he woke up famous. That fame never let him go, either. It always asked questions of him that he wasn't prepared to answer in a way that satisfied. It was an "either you get it or you don't and if you don't, well, sorry, buddy but that's on you." Only that perspective is one that has been honed to a fine edge by The Beatles and Andy Warhol and every Punk rocker and bad-boy actor and Madonna and Pink and so on, since then. Kerouac wanted to be Hemingway, only not so much. Hemingway showed us that even he didn't want to be Hemingway after a while. So did Jack Kerouac. Fame is a suckish thing - it feeds on everything but provides little sustenance back to us. And when so many people make a living giving and taking away fame with something resembling sleight of hand, or as an inside joke, it seems a terrible price to pay for being good at something.

I've said a few times before that there are moments and events that you ought to experience at the right time and in the right order. I tried to get my girls to read Tolkien before Harry Potter – failed. Ah, well. On the other hand, I took them fishing before ever playing video games. More seriously, they had good math teachers, early on, before learning it became an emotional Stonewall. And they ate peanut butter sandwiches long before trying a McDonald's hamburger, to their everlasting good fortune as we sat at home during quarantine this spring and summer.

I was lucky. I read On The Road at precisely the right time in my life, and I highly recommend that anyone eighteen or so, skinny and longing to be in love, looking but not desperately for that task that they will perform for a while in their life (what we used to call "the rest of our life" but that ship has sailed,) unhappy but not despairing, with some fast friends but not many, and a long weekend ahead of them, also read this book. Get your own copy, mark it up with circled passages and margin comments and notes. It will stick to your ribs like a good meal, and you'll remember it, and the feeling it gave you for a long time, and that feeling will be there when you need to draw on it from time to time. If you are older, or don't have any concerns as mentioned above, are a social butterfly or the leader of an enormous posse of pals, significant others come and go in your life with reckless abandon, and you see your life's path laid out before you like a fragrant carpet of flowers, leave the book on the shelf. It's not for you. Go read something else. Or, go play a video game. Not that there's anything wrong with that.

So I guess to some extent I'm saying I'm glad I was born when I was, and that means being here now, which is no bed of roses. It's a bitch to need to do some of the things we're doing, and deal with some of the things we're dealing with. And, of course, some of those things are worse than others and I'm not saying that I have it more or less difficult than anyone else. Only you know how hard it is for you.

I don't apologize for loving On The Road. Yes, it's not a good read anymore. In my mind's memory-ear, it's much more beautiful than on the page before me today. And it's horribly sexist and full of all kinds of other 'isms, but there you are. I'm not sorry that I wanted to have such an odyssey in my life, a search for...what did Todd Rundgren call it - "Something? Anything?" I'm not sorry that I was a child once, and had to grow up somehow, make mistakes, study subjects that had nothing at all to do with a potential career. I would never want to be one of those who followed a life-syllabus. I am glad that I ran away once or twice, came back with some comprehension of the point of being here at all.

Static (Hermaneutics) – November 2020

I try not to spend too much time ruminating over what crosses my news radar. I exist with a combination of exhaustion and tinnitus – where my emotional ear just can't listen to all the yelling anymore. Yes, it could be said that I have become a slack bastard, no longer fully and appropriately connected with the minutiae. You'll get no apology from me for that. It's a noisy world, seemingly even more so than when I was younger, I think, and much of it is so because there are so very many microphones and each one is attached to so many speakers to pass on the noise.

I feel we have an unfortunate tendency to imagine that everything needs to be rewound and played again, sometimes running the same tape over the recording heads so that we amplify the words, making them seem more credentialled and therefore more true. That is, of course, a fallacy. Things can't be more true. They are only true, or false. Adding the emotion of increased volume doesn't make anything helpful, or true. Repetition doesn't either. Misunderstanding helps not at all.

In Noisy World, so many of us have an urge to be heard, published, read, cited, liked, hearted, starred. We want to be acknowledged. So we crank up the volume another notch and increase the frequency of our messages. Whatever we think at the moment. Repeating the loudest thing we just heard, we cock an ear into the reverberating tumult in the desperate hope of receiving some kind of analytics about our action. Hello! Hello… hello….

And when there is so much clutter, so much…amplitude, if you will…that which is shouted the most may be all that gets heard. And having been heard, the *louderthing* is the only thing that gets repeated by those who hear it. (In an obscure way, this makes me think about how barnacles somehow adhere to shoreline rocks where waves incessantly crash. How, I ask, can they hold on? Desperation is the answer.) People who are hungry for information will cling frantically to whatever they hear. They may or may not grapple with the ideas that information contains, but will merely echo it into the ether, for the same reasons mentioned above. And think how children hear their parents, their teachers, their friends, the noise around them, and repeat what they hear, sometimes with unfortunate consequences.

I recently saw a post in one of the social-media platforms from a person, a writer I assume, who suggested that literary magazines should go the way of the dodo-bird. That their time was past, and their "services" no longer necessary. Writers should, alternatively, post their writing in their own websites, blogs, walls, pages, channels, what have you. And readers can just read what they want. Without addressing the poster's concerns (I don't know what they are – perhaps one too many rejections, or just a general malaise for the whole submission/consideration/rejection or publication-iarchy,) I wonder if this may be something the writing and reading world is slipping towards, and if it is as misguided as it seems. What is the root-cause of such a perspective? Is it the natural inclination of writers to work in a vacuum, with only their cognitive biases to support them? Disappointment of some sort? A lack of trust in tools that can be hoarded and guarded by the profit-makers? Or a lost confidence in curation?

We'll see, and then we'll know. Maybe that day is coming. The hunger, resentment, the opportunistic availability of tools - I find no energy to be stridently against such a confluence of events. I can only go on reading, writing, thinking, watching...

Definition – December 2020

I know it's only November second, so please forgive me for not knowing with exactitude how the world has taken shape. I'm still in the thick of waiting and wondering what is going to happen, and what will happen after that. I trust that you already know, for good or bad, depending on your bent.

At the moment it's cold outside, but I still enjoy going out on the front porch with a good book and a cup of coffee, rapidly cooling, so that occasionally I must return to the kitchen to jostle the molecules in the microwave oven. I've recently finished reading the novel "Year of Wonders" by the terrific author Geraldine Brooks. If you have read any of her work, you know what I mean when I say that her attention to rhetorical detail is peerless, and if you haven't read anything by her, well, *go*. Do not wait. Download, purchase, borrow, acquire by any means necessary, her novels. It is not my intention, however, to do a book review. Better minds than mine do such things, and I think we are all better off because they do. We don't have to agree with everything they write, but at the very least they curate the works for us. We owe book reviewers thanks for taking on that task.

Rather I would like to talk about the word "nick." In Ms Brooks' novel, she provides us with a lesson in word-history, in etymology, with this little snippet of a word. Nick. How do we understand it nowadays? Nick is what we do when we shave too carelessly – chip out a bit of our flesh with the blade. I also wonder if it has some relation to the French word "niche" which means a small recess carved out of a wall, for a statue or some other decorative object. Nick is also one of those terms that is a strange reversal on itself. The word 'nickname' currently means an alternative to someone's given appellation, usually something shorter, easier to say, affectionate. Nick from Nicholas, for example. But supposedly it originates in the term "eke-name," with *eke* coming from the Old English for "a part added on." Which still makes a certain sense, as nicknames don't replace names, but are additional ways of referring to someone. Terms of familiarity or affection, derision or jest. My mom, for example, called me Garry most of the time, except when I was in trouble for eating all of the semi-sweet morsels she'd bought to bake something. Then it was the more formal *Garrison*, and when I heard that I knew that her wrath was about to descend on me, for any number of legitimate reasons.

So, is a nick a removal or an addition? I guess that depends on your point of view.

But it's also a slang term in British vernacular meaning anything from stealing to where you go if you're caught stealing. I like that (not the stealing, but how the single slang incorporates all of functionality.) Nick (steal) something, you get nicked (arrested), and sent to the nick (prison). And, if you look at Ms Brooks' work, in particular the episodes about mining, and I'm not going to take away the fun of your reading her book, but I think you will see that the online dictionaries and wiktionaries may have this wrong, or at least confused. Nick isn't a nineteenth century term, but a bit of the daily language from much, much earlier. In other words, the usage of the well-morph'd slang might feel like it belongs in *My Fair Lady* or *Mary Poppins*, but the term itself goes back to… *A Man for All Seasons*.

Somewhat tangentially, it seems to me that when we speak or write we have a tendency to merge the meanings of words together, to treat them as interchangeable synonyms in our minds. Take, for example, dread, apprehension, anxiety and anticipation. Are they similarly defined in the everyday dictionary of our minds? I suppose. But the truth is quite different. The etymology of "dread" is Old English - the fear of something that we think is coming. Anticipation's root meaning, on the other hand, is the Latin "taken before," or to be aware of something coming before it gets here. Apprehension, on yet another hand, is seizing an idea of something – in effect grasping what is coming. And in anxiety we have the Latin for *to trouble* and the Greek for *choke*.

The nuances are there. Anticipation? An awareness of something out there, in the future, known or unknown. Dread is fear of that unknown future. Apprehension is grasping at that future even before it arrives. And anxiety, the sense that the future is trouble indeed, sent to…take our ability to breathe.

I appreciate that the word choices give us clarity, specificity of idea. That we don't always communicate that way? I suppose I get it. The world is urgent, loud, confusing. It doesn't always give us the extra moments to collect our thoughts. We need to talk to each other, ask questions. We need to really listen to the answers. If we don't understand, well, step forward and ask more questions. Don't give up.

Thoughts About Endings and Beginnings – January 2021

It's always a difficult trick for me to finally put down my pen (metaphorically) and have the congratulatory drink and cigarette (also metaphorical!) when working a writing project and reaching those words "The End." I've asked other writers, and they tend to have a pat answer to my question. *Oh, yeah, it just ends*, they tell me, or they have had it outlined since the start and so it's just a small matter of connecting the verbal dots. I don't believe them, of course. Ending is always a bitch.

Why is that, do you suppose?

Ending is defined as that never quite perfect point between utter confusion for your reader as to why they ran out of pages to read but don't understand what happened and the glazed look in their eyes when the typing continues but the point in reading on is lost.

I mean, we're supposed to be storytellers – and when the story is over, isn't that all there is? Or when there is nothing more, don't we stop telling the yarn. Cease the regaling? *Oh, wait, I forgot about…this is funny…I've left something…add that on.* Tweaking, nudging, polishing, revisiting. All of those thoughts, yes, but they are not my only concerns. There's a bigger thing going on here. Part of that is ending includes giving something up. Surrendering it to others. Releasing it to the wild, so to speak. And just as troubling is ending means not doing it anymore. Doing something, but not this.   Ending is about moving on. And moving on is not easy for some folks.

Most people.

Well, more specifically, all of us so-called creative types who fiddle with things until they are finally snatched out of our hands.

Here's my not very original theory: ending is not the same as finishing. Completing a race is finishing. Finishing a meal is not the same. The difference, you say, may be only slight – a nuance of interpretation. Maybe.

Ending never goes well, does it? Relationships? No. School years? Administrations? No. Binge-watched costume dramas? Hell, no.

Another *why* question: why can we finish meals (knowing we can start another in a few hours, if we ate all of our vegetables), but have a hard time ending the writing of a story or poem, even though we know (implicitly) that we can begin scribing another if we are so inclined. And, yes, I am fully aware that writing a poem is three degrees of difficulty greater than swallowing a serving of lima beans, but I hope you get my point.

I say yes, with hesitation. I could be wrong.

There is a great deal of wheel-spinning when I begin something new. Launching sentences somewhere other than the story's beginning. I find achieving narrative traction seems to require it - I don't know about you. On the other hand, I have a friend that begins with the best of them, can scribble page after page of...*preamble*, and then consistently rides completely off the rails. He can't find plot development on a map, has no middle game, won't defend the premise or give the characters permission to move from their opening positions, as if it is a chess game with no timeclock. Instead, he just keeps describing the whole world, and all of the people in it.

Character development is good, don't get me wrong, but providing more character description (I was just about to write "…than is necessary" but of course if they must do it to get past this sort of 'block" then it's necessary, isn't it?) is just as big a non-starter as my own wandering off-topic and creating side-stories that often need to be polished away in rewrite.

Another theory: that the false-start is something that can be fixed in rewrite, but the inability to end is that which prevents rewrite. Ah-ha! Is that inability to end of which we speak a ruse to keep from having to set the story aside and, when it has fermented appropriately, begin the rewrite? Or do writers not enjoy the act of ending a story because it leads to having to start the next? Do they dislike beginning because it inevitably proceeds towards another bit of heartbreak?

Have I pursued this line of questionable reasoning longer than I should?

Stop.

I want to talk about what I want to talk about! – February 2021

It is a current bone of contention (with me) here at home that we talk a lot, but not very often is it about something I'm interested in discussing. It's my fault, I know. After all, things are happening on *Next Door*. Someone said something to someone else on the most recent phone call or binge-watched drama, but I was a participant in neither, so there is no contextual thread I can latch on to. There's also the news on TV, but everyone is exhausted with the stress-filled minutiae that a twenty-four-hour news cycle brings, so we're at loose ends with regards to that. It seems to be programmed to eventually enrage, so I find myself walking away when the television is on for that reason.

I sit a lot and read. I scribble, then empty the dishwasher. Walk upstairs, because it's there, and therefore needs investigating, in the same way that cats wander around a house, peering around corners and under beds. If I bump into my wife or daughters, I don't interrupt them, because I don't know what they're doing and I want to respect any privacy of thought or action they may require in their day. I sit in the bedroom and read something different – my chairs are pre-set with a small stack of books beside them. I hum a song while I read until it annoys even me.

At prescribed, or is it proscribed, moments during the day we interrupt one another with "what's for lunch?" or "what do you want for dinner?" I don't know. The inevitable quadrant-chart of questions: What are my choices? Am I cooking? When do you want to eat? What are you hungry for? All leading to the place in a relationship everyone is familiar with – why are you asking me? Just make something.

Meals are fixed, we sit and eat. The talk is about today's accomplishments or failures, what might or might not happen tomorrow or the next day. I have no plans, have done little of note this day (so far) and have nothing to offer. I listen, but it seems to me that it isn't important that I do, or maybe it is and I just don't know how. I mean, I know how to listen, but should I?

Well, we burn up time, and energy, and that's something. Something good? I can't say. Does it put wear and tear on us? You bet. We want to be civil to each other, but this is hard. Lockdown, prolonged, has taken a toll on our sensibilities. We eat early, or late. Salads and sliced fruit. Comments include how good this is for our overall health. Sometimes we skip a meal. So it goes, as the great man said.

I am not looking the gift horse in the mouth, I swear. It is a blessing that we can stay home, as safe as that allows us to be, and let the world bring the bare necessities to us and then some. I have a lifetime supply of fig newtons in one cupboard and nine pounds of peanut butter, so if there's a land war in Asia I'm good for the first few battles. One daughter is in school in my office downstairs, learning organic chemistry. Holy crap, right? The other has an apartment, where this fall she taught herself to crochet while discussing push-and pull marketing strategy in B2B campaigns on Zoom. She'll graduate this summer and we've talked about grad school and internships and she's so much smarter than I am that I feel like she's going to reach over at some point and pat me on the head and say 'there, there. That's a good Dad."

I am reliably informed (those are trigger words, yeah?) that this will all end at some time in the reasonable future, as such things are measured. I have work to do, creating in the ineffable vacuum of my own making. I can hang in there for a while longer. (Who am I kidding? – this is my wheelhouse. Having very limited human contact is one of my best things. Hey, would you like to talk about my WIP? Got a minute? Can I read something to you?)

Midwinter Tid-bits – March 2021

I'm sitting in my office, staring at the keyboard. Quite certain that I want to say something, but not so sure of what I want to say. Does this ever happen to you? Finding yourself a technological variant of tongue-tied? What do you do to overcome that hurdle? Do you step away from the keyboard, put the computer in sleep-mode and do something else until you can find the starting point? Perhaps you tug out a composition notebook and make lists instead: groceries you need this week. Books you've promised yourself to read. Or do you catch up on your administrative duties? Clear the inbox, so to speak. Sit back down and determinedly send out all those emails you've been promising. Or are all of these things terribly clear flags that reveal my age. Wow, you're old, you're thinking. Everything you just talked about are things I never do.

Yeah, I'm older than I was this time last year. More than is normal, whatever that means. I forget what that's called, aging faster than your chronological age. An existential hiccup in relativity, where your face still looks good but your hands and neck give you away. In actuality, my neck isn't something I can even see. I stopped trimming my beard just after Thanksgiving – I mean winter was coming and I needed to work on my sword-handling. Yes, I was behind on that mangled pop-reference, too. It's my approach to the world that is the tell-tale. I'm four or five of the seven dwarfs: grumpy, sleepy, dopey, hesitant and attitudinal.

Am I watching too much television? Probably. I have the time, after all, and what better use for time than to waste it? At the moment, I'm letting a manuscript *ferment* – that moment in time you give something you've written before you come back and shred it-edit it (say that five times fast.) How else can you work up the courage to murder your darlings? I've started something new, and it smacks of the thing I just finished, so I don't have a lot of confidence in it. So I'm mostly…uninvolved, right now. There's no sitting in coffee-shops perusing Facebook. No walking up and down the grocery aisles seeing what canned vegetables are on special. No more flipping back and forth between the news-outlets to see who's more unhinged. And I don't do most of the other social media and communication tools that are available out there in the app-verse. I've been specifically instructed by my daughters to avoid Instagram and Snap-chat, for reasons that apparently don't require explanation, because they have provided none. And suffice to say, Tik-Tok's popularity eludes me.

I always assumed that when I hit an age-benchmark like…wherever the hell I am at the moment, I would be recognized by my choice of shoes, or the indelible deli-mustard stains on my shirt. I thought I would go gently into that good night humming along with something or other from the playlist in my head and young people would think "whoa, way to jam, old man." Ironically.

But it seems that I'm slip-sliding away, technologically. This past year I ignored so much in the interest of my WIP that I missed out on what a *subreddit* is. And a *substack*. And *sub-smash*. Don't even mention any sub without real tuna. Frankly, at the moment, anything with the prefix "sub" in it is not my favorite. Subdural Hematoma comes to mind.

I feel like what's happening is that things are mutating so quickly that I'm always about forty-five minutes behind. I'm late, hopping on the following train, the uncool one, the one that stops at every station and gets me to work tardy no matter that I have a seat and my ticket is transferrable. What is the cure for this? How can I get back into the mix? Why do I even want to get back in the mix? What is wrong with me?

Take a breath, fella. Go outside and walk around the block. You're not getting old, you're acting old.

And let me clarify: I'm not…worried about becoming my parents. I'm neither smart enough to be very much like them, nor have I had the serious world-experience that they did to form me into someone worthy of being part of the greatest generation, if you follow that sort of naming convention. I have, however, an observational curiosity about my own development along the way and find it interesting that my musical tastes lean toward the bookends – Steely Dan and…Billie Eilish – something, I think, that a therapist might be able to wheedle loose from my cerebrum, but I'm not going there. I mean, you know, into a doctor's office. I don't have a hazmat suit, but I do wear an old olive-green Navy coat and a scarf, and my mask. Although by the time you read this, it may be summer again. Perhaps I need a different mask, something with Edwardian florals on it. Yes, that's just the thing.

Nothing To Say – April 2021

I may have already mentioned this: I play a game, online, on my phone, with many other players worldwide, and the starting object is one thing (to clobber zombies) and then over time the game becomes another thing (to make alliances and fight other players). And for what it's worth to any armchair analysts, I choose not to be in an alliance. I prefer just to collect resources and fight the program-created zombies. I do get attacked from time to time, but I don't keep my treasure out there to be the spoils of war. I use what I gather and then go get more. I suspect that there is a dissatisfaction in an "opponent" checking out my camp and seeing little of value there. Perhaps because of this there are players who think twice before making the effort to attack me. Perhaps not. We are an aggressive species, whether we like to admit it or not.

And so the game goes. A lot like life. Occasionally I move… forward, one slow ladder-rung level at a time, and that's something. The levels have meaning in the bigger plot of the game, but not much to me. But it helps me play my own game. Occasionally, I'm involved in a battle I didn't instigate in any way other than just being in the app, on the board, so to speak, with my camp and level displayed for others to investigate. I treat a battle like the weather – a hurricane or tsunami - cleaning up after with the resignation that this, too, is part of life.

Still, I may have learned something in recent days that intrigues me. I think there is another game going on, within the game, something altogether unexpected and interesting to me. A function provided by the game developers permits players to chat with one another during the zombie-hunt. Ostensibly, it is a tool that provides people who don't really know each other (I assume) a way to ask for assistance, to lend each other resources, or rally troops for a major undead-clobbering campaign, or to deal with one of the special events that the game introduces once or twice a month – holiday-themed rewards or alliance-vs-alliance strength tests, intended to add to the game experience – the aggressive part. Leaders of alliances can speak, via text, to their members and subjects, and each other, to coordinate their movements.

But beneath all of the game stuff, this old-school chatroom is a social media platform, for communication among players, and not just during the "specials," but all of the time. Players log on to see what others are doing, while they collect resources and kill zombies and other enemies. They ask personal questions, get answers, talk to and tease each other about how they play the game. And they learn about one another, the conversations they have are revelatory, and the friendships seem to be as important as playing the game itself. Players sign on and call out for friends to see if they're out there. They talk about what they've been doing that day, and what they might do later – in this "public" place. They josh, they console, they flirt. It is a kind of like-minded community.

None of this should be surprising, to you or to me. Or my friend John, who often says to me that I need to try to get to my points with greater celerity. Which I agree. But not at this particular moment.

What is most interesting to me is that there is a sort of briefhand they use – like something I learned about in middle-school for taking notes during class. The elimination of certain rules of language and the addition of others, and possibly unique to this game and its long-term players. Replacement of words with emojis – quite common in our electronic social interaction and the construction of other pictures from keyboard characters –

dashes, emdashes, dots, dashes and slashes, into pictures that portray an interpretable message. I suspect that the pidgin that they have created is tops-down – the most senior players who have known each other as allies and opponents the longest, make the rules for what typing in all caps represents, or what one pair of emoji googly-eyes means versus two or even three. Does it mean "look" or "look!" or "LOOK!" and if so, what is the message. With words, glyphs and pictograms, repetition, and a kind of learned nuance of response timing and non-response, a shared jargon-code has been invented or selectively pulled from other social environments by the players and agreed to as *creole* – a new mother-tongue for this game in which I am a foreigner. I can kibbitz this public "party line" and find doing so easily more fascinating than the game itself.

What is it am I seeing? A possible mutation to our language, in which the lush vocabulary of English is altered, for whatever reason – expedience, privacy, playfulness – into something else. Will there be clarity? Will there be a musical quality to it, a poetry that arises from some sort of phoenix ash of grammar and structure that I understand? Or is this already there, and I am not seeing, or able to interpret it because I'm not worthy to be its Champollion or Turing?

When we speak to one another in person there is a linguistic understanding between us, an agreed to set of guidelines. We use the same language, for example, or some common tongue. When we switch to the telephone, those precise guidelines cannot and therefore do not apply. On the telephone, we cannot use our faces - our body-language - to temper our words into comprehension by the person we are speaking with. Some of this possibly tele-miscommunication (a hundred *years* of it, for crying out loud) has been partially rectified by tools – Skype, Facetime and Zoom – but not completely. Still, there is still breakage in the line-speeds and screen-sizes that frustrate, disappoint, subtly change the mood of the conversation.

These tools of the 21st century assume that people want to be understood by others, by everyone. We feel a need to have as much social context in our business as we can, particularly in times of isolation such as that which we currently experience. But what if this were not the case? What if the senior players of my game – belay that, *their* game – don't necessarily care that I understand them. I am still, to them, a novice, a newb who has not met the coming-of-age requirements of their social conventions. I am an outsider. They, on the other hand, are a tribe of friends and acquaintances, with rituals and social hierarchies to which I am intentionally not privy. They don't ask me to leave, don't exclude me, but they don't welcome me, either.

And, as a final note, players are also required to occasionally "war" with one another, tribe versus tribe, and then band together as a clan of tribes to war against other clans. These ritualized wars have a prescribed length, at which the clans and tribes return to a state of peace. Oddly enough, the players feel no enmity towards each other before or after these ritual-was. War is just the passing of treasure from one to another, and the earning of experience-treasure from the game-developers – the Gods? The players open their chatrooms to the greater group, beyond their tribes and clans and josh and console and flirt some more, in their word-and-picture secret code. It's all part of the game, I've been told on more than one occasion. And that, too, is interesting to me. Maybe there's something more here than meets the eye.

Syzygy – May 2021

As you who have been reading for a while may already have surmised, I am fascinated with language. I appreciate the vastness of the English vocabulary, and the nuance and selection offered to us, when we choose to read or talk or write. And I certainly don't consider it pompous or elitist to use the available resource. In truth, I find it wasteful to leave words on the table in lieu of using pictures and glyphs in our daily communications with each other. Bad enough that we select nipped and tucked thought-lets to begin with, often someone else's, I fear that for many reasons our year-long physical separation one from another has further edited our communication habits, reducing our patience for what is often disparagingly called long-windedness.

And that appellation certainly belongs to me. I've been on Zoom calls – friends getting together regularly or book-studies or with my daughters, and I frequently have to rein myself in. No one, I have deduced, wants to hear anybody unload all of the baggage they carry. We just don't have the stamina, or like anyone quite that much. Oh, we may love them and deeply, but that's asking a lot. My wife knows that, and uses the ploy of falling asleep when I go off on tangent after tangent answering the question "what do you have on tap tomorrow?" My daughters, on the other hand, are kind and treat me as they would, say, a wet dog they found begging at the door. *Who's a good boy?*

And so here's your last warning to turn the page before I regale you with something I found recently. It has to do with the word with which I've entitled this ramble. The term "syzygy." Here's how it's defined from a cut-and-pasted online dictionary entry: 1. (Astronomy) either of the two positions (conjunction or opposition) of a celestial body when sun, earth, and the body lie in a straight line: the moon is at syzygy when full. 2. (Poetry) (in classical prosody) a metrical unit of two feet.

This fascinates me. Syzygy. From the Greek for yoke, union, conjunction. A word that has such divers meaning is a bit of a unicorn, and great fun. Let's unpack this. A common syzygy is the spring and neap tides caused by the sun, earth and moon being in syzygy (noticeable to us when the moon is full or new). The astronomy definition is laying out for us that the planets and the sun have their own elegance – they are behaving as they must, not with randomicity. That they can align as they follow their personal ellipses about the so-called center – the sun – reveals that rules are being followed. The harmony of the spheres, as it has been called, is that planets and stars have positioned themselves where they must be. They are right-distanced from one another, moving at the appropriate speed, spinning or not as they must. Evidence of their shifting over eons atop eons, plays this out.

What has this to do with poetry? Let's see. A poetic Syzygy is the alignment of two poetic feet, achieving an alliterative feeling to a phrase. You have to trust me on this. Go and dredge up your old Norton Anthology of Poetry and see for yourself. Whoever coined this term for poetic alignment was thinking about elegance, about the sensibility of this kind of stringing together of words, how well it worked for communicating beauty.

There is a third fragment of a definition that I left out. *Any rare pairing, usually of opposites*. A tempting tidbit: something to think about. And I think it is right that this should be included in our little semi-academic investigation. I'm no mathematician nor a poetic scholar, but for syzygy to work, I suspect, there must be as much push as pull. The celestial bodies align according to rules of mass and velocity, distance and time. Perhaps they even jiggle into place, like the tumblers of a lock do under the command of a very old key. And words? Endless combination, endless tension gained and released, to make the point.

And herein lies my own point. The truth as I see it, we risk losing the capacity to say what can be said, elegantly or otherwise. We don't take deep enough breaths, perhaps. Everything seems to be a *bark*, a dog saying something in one short and mighty woof, and the rest of us only passing that message on down the lane and around the corner.

Make the big statements, say I. Ramble on. Go on a diatribe. I'm with you, along for the ride, seatbelt fastened. Play with structure, be somewhat difficult to follow. Occasionally veer off into the deep weeds.

And while you're at it – think about this, just for fun: Syzygy is the shortest word in the English language that, when written in cursive, lower-case, has five letters that drop below the line. Five of six, to be precise. Check it out: *syzygy*

That's not your job – June 2021

I'm not a big fan of social media. I feel sometimes that it is akin to a traffic accident on the highway, a wildfire, one that we all stop our vehicles to watch, not noticing that it has slipped around behind and now threatens to consume us. And before you activate your righteous ire button, yes, I have a Twitter account, recognize the hypocrisy, and don't apologize for it. I can guess what you're thinking: What the hell?

Yeah. You're right. How can I badmouth the hand that feeds me?

Well, let me climb back up on my high horse and say it doesn't feed me. I have no illusion that it does me any good whatsoever. I don't sell books or get readers from it, create connections to useful others, or crowdsource…anything. If I ever thought I would gain some functional career boost from a free piece of software, I was misguided.

But my motives were sound. Thirty-five years ago, we were told that no one reads anymore. Scary times for me, because I did, receiving my Book of the Month Club catalog and making my choices according to a very stringent set of guidelines (how many can I afford and still keep my lights on?) I had a lovely little bookstore I also frequented, the Cranbury Bookworm, in Cranbury, New Jersey, a short bike ride from my home. It was an old house on the main street, with creaky stairs and shelves and stacks all cantilevered into corners and along walls. You can check it out – it's still there and I'll bet still has some hidden treasures going for a song.

And parenthetically, I was writing love poems and using company software and mainframe time to do layout and printing of little chapbooks of my work, to share with friends. They were lovely, awful, amazing things.

No one reads anymore. What would I do if books went away, or at least were difficult to find? What if only the big-name authors got published, and the New York Times Review of Books… didn't? How would we readers find the quirky, the obscure, the not-so-well-received?

Then, about thirty years ago, the publishing world (spoken as if it were a single, unified organism, with a snake head that could be cut off by some dragonslayer) altered itself to align with shiny new mega-bookstores, intended to take what was left of the industry and consolidate it some more, under the auspices of economies of scale profit-theory. Wait a minute – I thought nobody reads? Wrong. I signed up for membership discounts and made my Saturday afternoon journey to the mall and wandered the aisles, looking for paperback copies of bestsellers and seeking the below-cost copies of classics I was supposed to have read in high-school. If, perchance, print-matter was going away, I was going to have a stockpile of TBR that would last at least through the millennium, when all the power kicked off and we returned to a state of stone-aged grace. I also submitted my foolishly derivative sci-fi yarns to the pulp monthlies I picked up at the little newsstand next to the video rental store. I learned a lot about rejection, but who doesn't? I kept writing. I kept reading. What better way to approach the end of the world?

Twenty years ago? As I recall, the publishing giants – all reswizzled, rebranded, relaxing and basking in renewed sales of print matter discovered that the new little online bookstore named after a South American river wasn't going away. The megastores were sweating it, too, those that didn't understand the internet and what was possible. People spending their money online? Preposterous. And my little independent bookstores – the ones I could drive to and stand around in and talk with the booksellers and even the bookbuyers and find out what was cool out there, but wouldn't get much if any shelf space so if I wanted a copy they could order one for me – well, they…went away.

And only slightly tangentially, as publishing, reading and selling books sea-changed, the libraries massaged their game, too. My two locals (it is a wonder to belong to two public libraries, I must say) had a tough time, at first. What to stock on shelves. What to borrow from other libraries, if they can, so that everyone doesn't have to spend the bucks on the same, rarely read items. There's a certain kind of magic in a library. I highly recommend knowing a few librarians, and treating them with respect.

How do you even browse online? Algorithms of previous interests are not the same. Telling me what others did in my position is not the same. Browsing is defined as surveying goods in a leisurely and casual way. Allowing me to type in keywords for a search is something, but not the same as shelf space, isles of titles, authors, subject matter. If you can't see what's out there, how do you include them in your "survey?" That's always been my problem with the big river store. At least in a megastore, I could look around. I can't do that same thing online. And I am in an albeit fortunate position that I can go to my last small handful of independent bookstores, look for what interests me, and purchase them without too much of a discount. It may or may not make a difference in the end. But I'm hopeful.

I'm pretty old school about this, with all of the "please shut up" that phrase deserves. I keep returning to the refrain: do your job. That's not your job. If you are a writer, you should be writing, not trying to build a following by working up a lather navigating Twitter to locate like-minded smiley-face emoji bearers, hoping that someone has some skill you can barter for, or makes purchase decisions based on recommendations from strangers (and I mean that term in every way it can be defined.)

Here are my top five reasons for not liking the tools everyone claims to use to stay connected.

1) We let connections extend beyond our actual friendships.
2) We listen to all the noise without having the tools to filter it.
3) We request and take advice from people when we wouldn't normally do so.
4) We make it our creative outlet.
5) We take the bait – respond to the shouting, let that be our mood-du-jour.

That's a lot to unpack. Hand me the bolt cutters, let's snap open that lock.

Not being able to differentiate between friends and acquaintances, friends and people you cannot avoid running into at work and in the world, friends and neighbors, is not good. Not good at all. I'm not going to try to define "friend" for you, but at its simplest, a friend is someone who will put up with you. And if you were walking with Dante through the gates of level-one hell, you would finally admit to yourself that this is a lot to ask of anyone. A friend is someone you have time for – and let's get this out of the way, no one has enough time for anything anymore. Our lives are cluttered. We are all hoarders of one type or another (and are all appalled at everyone else's hoarding!) Except for your friends, who for reasons defying explanation, think you're pretty great, and want to spend that time they have with you. So, as we used to say *go figure*.

All of those other people in your "feed" are talking, getting in the way of the messages from your…real friends, and so you're "hearing" all the talking and giving it similar weight to the words of your friends. That can't be good, can it? So sometimes you need help with something and throw that request for information out into the 'verse and advice does come back. And you park it in your brain in a file called "advice from friends." But is it? Would you take advice from the cashier at the local gas-&-sip? Yes, the one where you bought the powdered donuts that were so old they had a Stegosaurus on the package. The part that's weird to me is that all of those folks – let's call them…strangers – have real friends, too, that they should be talking to, listening to, and not talking and listening to you. Nor you to them.

And it's all done under the auspices of friendly banter. In whose best interests is all this conversing, stranger to stranger? No one. Well, no one we know. What is needed at this point is a filter. Something that returns our online "conversations" to behaving like live ones. You know, those moments over the dinner table when no one would think of saying *the horror, the horror!*

Getting stuff done – July 2021

I am told that it's been four hundred forty-four or so days since the beginnings of Covid Lockdown back in 2020, and we're not locked down so much anymore – although I do not know what the world has in store for us by the time this is posted, or when you read it – and I'd like to say something. I am also told that to write about this at this point is dog-piling, or boring or something of that ilk. Which is not my intention. I would rather talk about writing. Which I have been doing a great deal of since four hundred forty-five days ago. Put down "on paper" (an archaic term, yes? Who still prints anything out to get a better view?) the first draft of a novel, set it aside, started another and as of today I'm about two-thirds of the way through it, I think.

To what do I owe this burst of creative energy? Creative angst? Is it that uncomplicated – in times of difficulty, we have the need to create – to leave something, a trail of breadcrumbs for us to find our way back to normal or a trail of breadcrumbs for our rescuers to find us as we become lost in the existential forest?

Wait – that was kind of complicated.

I don't know how it is for you, but I try to sit down at the desk and write each and every day. Some days more than others are very productive in a linear sort of way – the work-in-progress gets more added on where I left off last time. In my case it's my first-person narrator trying to come to grips with his first "experience" in young love. Or something like young love, but is mostly the abject terror of being in a teenaged body with a teenaged brain trying to run things, and mostly he gets asked questions like what are you thinking and he's got nothing to say. Because that's how I remember it. It's not a memoir – because that would be deeply messed up at this point in my actual life –

but more like putting what I remember of my seventeen year old self placed in situations I can only thank the gods I didn't have to deal with, and what might I have done in those very fictional situations.

Write about what you know? Oh, horseshit. Write about what you feel.

And some days this works brilliantly. Other days are more like chipping away at a block of granite. I look for a point of entry, find it and burrow in to see what I can say about it. I don't get up from the desk and walk away (although I do sometimes get up and walk around, ruminating about plot arc or the lack thereof, or ask my characters what happens next, spinning in ever widening circles until the path becomes clearer in the fog.

And that is why lockdown has been my wheelhouse. I couldn't go to the store for a loaf of rustic French bread, couldn't take a break and go see a movie (well, not any farther than the living room), couldn't wander over to a friend's house and bug them, when they should be writing, too…. I did carry a (paper) notebook out on the front porch and scribble in the glare for a little while, from time to time, which counted as something accomplished even if it was off WIP topic and ended up a poem about missing going to the grocery store and will we ever have the woman in the back of the supermarket making pigs-in-a-blanket dipped in home-made barbecue sauce on toothpicks again? What if pigs-in-a-blanket dipped in barbecue sauce is a cure? How do you know? Did anyone even check? I did convert my files to online documents that I could share with my occasionally short-tempered beta readers – who have shown the patience of Job with my loss of internal clock and calendar. Yes, I sent messages at the wrong time of day, the wrong days of the week and then followed up with calls to ask if my messages had been received and what was the answer? Yes, I sent a graphomaniacal (is that even a thing?) amount of content to folks who had better things to do than keep me informed about the viability of my story line and sketchiness of character development. What's the old saying – friends will read your prose; good friends help you murder your darlings. And, no, you shouldn't test friendships during a global anything.

So I am getting back out in the world – a little slowly because I like it here at my desk. I like the little space I've carved out, with books behind me and a comfortable chair in front of me (you know, when I need a nap because writing is desperately hard work.) I like that there's coffee almost 7 X 24 in this joint and what my younger daughter calls "Oreo knock-offs" on a shelf over the fridge should I get peckish. I like how one of my characters is a teacher that's a knock-off of my Dad, and he's a funny sort with a bad haircut who understands the rough patch some teenagers go through.

I hope that you've been safe and productive and that you're reading this in a place you love.

Vacuum – August 2021

Here's something that's been weighing on my mind lately: How do you know if you're a good writer? How do you keep going, when some of the feedback you receive (in particular, from yourself, but also that vague and general negativity known as "rejection") is not good? I'm a loner already – sitting at my desk, typing. Keeping to the plan, that this work-in-progress is something worthy of pursuit and hoping that the ideas for what happens next will continue to flow.

Writers are forced by the nature of the beast, the gravitational pull of the moon, the second Law of Thermodynamics, what have you, to be optimists. Which is pretty tricky, considering that in some ways we work in a vacuum. Actually, lately – last year, I mean - a vacuum within a vacuum, something I don't even know is possible, and whether it's worse or better. Sort of like when a bully uses your hand to smack your face, over and over, asking the question "why are you hitting yourself?" It has to be better than the bully actually pummeling you, right? Being locked down inside a lockdown? Damn.

So, how do I define "optimists?" Well, those who sit and type (or scrawl) our words and use the goals called "good" or "not so good, but still something…," while at the same time adding the layer of "productive," to the mix, all while having "publishable" and "valuable" barking at us at the end of their leads. And we've very little idea if anything we do accomplishes those measurements. Oh, we may have a peanut gallery of friends and relations who suffer our semi-constant "can I read this to you?" We compare our work to the writing we like (or even the writing we don't), pulled off our bookshelves, and pat or flagellate our backs correspondingly. We form nebulous "writing groups," in the hopes that someone, someday, will make contact and we can all escape together off that island. And social media permits a sort of pick-your-poison, proceed at your own risk kind of wild west-passive aggressive feedback clusterfuck, if that's what you're in to. Roll that all together, let it proof for a while, bake it, and then ask someone else to please, eat, and that's how I define optimists.

Mostly, though, we live in our own heads. And behind our closed doors where we crank up the music and bang our heads against the wall as much as we tip-tap on the keyboard. And walking around the neighborhood, noodling about characters and sub-plots and how to include something we read months ago when we were researching home-made crystalized ginger root or the determining of white blood cell counts or how fantastic are holy mountains in Sri Lanka. We muddle through. That's what we're considering when we tell others that writing is fun. Love it! Not the something like anguish of not being able to think of a synonym for migraine headache or the name of that city on the spur of the bootheel of Italy, you know, the one that sticks out into the glittering, azure water of the Adriatic. Even using an online map. Where the hell is that city? That part of writing is fun in the same way that a hangnail, a hangover, or hanging off a cliff by one hand is fun, as in something between not very much and not at all.

That's when we wish there were bleachers full of fans who want to help, like in baseball. Like standing in right-field, everyone in the stadium holding a free beer in one hand and a pencil in the other, ready to give an assist to a long fly ball of a sentence that's gotten out of control and beginning to seem like there is no such thing as punctuation and periods and *speelchock* or even new paragraphs because the wind has gotten beneath the wing and is lifting the whole plane up into something resembling the ionosphere where there is no air and the writer is losing consciousness and if someone doesn't do something soon, what will become of him? Or her?

Or, is that just me? All I want is something helpful. It doesn't seem like very much to ask.

Winding Down my Stay-At-Home-Dad gig – September 2021

My eldest and I have found a time of day that works particularly well for us to converse. She likes to call me at night, just before she goes to bed. 11:45 is a very good part of the evening. Not quite tired, no more snacks, the last ballgame scores coming in, I've sent my video-game troops out to collect tomorrow's resources (see my notes on playing a MMP online game in the April 2021 essay) and then the phone rings and it is she.

We talk about, well…whatever she wants to talk about. Sometimes she's exhausted with school and her internship work and navigating the not-quite-post-anything world. It is just as likely that she asks me how my writing went on this day or the weather or some tidbit she picked up in class and wants to know if I ever heard this before. We talk about relationships, how to keep them, how to fix them, what makes them thrive. We discuss the climate (of everything – social, political, and of course the planet's.) And then she might just as likely ask me about word-choices in marketing and how much it is like writing poetry, or she'll let me read to her a raw and manic paragraph or two of my day's work. It is here, in the dim, beige light of a single overhead lamp in my office, that I recognize that this is my audience. Not just any young-twenties person, but my person. When I get up in the morning and sit down at my keyboard, it is she I am trying to make laugh. The perceived she – sitting across from me and drinking a cup of yesterday's coffee, creamed and sugared and reheated in the microwave, her feet up and eyes closed, just listening. And the real her, miles away, leaning on her old desk, staring at me with a crooked smile as I read. So, here comes a funny part, or a passage I intended to be funny. We'll see. I am hopeful, don't telegraph the moment, keep reading, my voice even. But she snorts and is laughing and waves her hands and tells me to go back and pick it up again. Say the funny part again, Dad. And that's why I write, and why I go on. I've been paid by laughter from my audience. My person. It's a heck of a thing.

She signs off to go to sleep, and I pad upstairs and check on my younger daughter, who is soon to be off into her second year of college, and first on campus. Her light is on. Her laptop glows in her face. Don't stay up too late, I tell her, and she promises, which is both polite and a bit silly, in that although we've tried to stay out of her business because she has spent the school year at home, doing it all remotely and well, yet we still get in her business. She is patient with me. Always tells me how she thinks she's done on a test. (My god, she's taking Organic Chemistry, about which I know nothing.) Sometimes, when we are simultaneously puttering around in the kitchen, I occasionally ask if she needs help opening something, a child-proof package or ornery jar. *No, Dad, I've got it*, is her response. I know what she means – the throwaway shorthand that implies "thanks for offering, but whatever I'm doing that seems like I'm not doing it will be done in just a moment, so, no." I also know what she doesn't mean: I've outgrown you, Dad. Nevertheless, I have told her that soon she will need to remember to call me from school, because I will miss having her around and sitting on the porch and drinking tea and opening her mayonnaise and watching Japanese anime with subtitles and she has carefully explained to me that we can do this sharing thing on our computers so it'll be like we're both still watching together and whoever invented that technology *thank you very much*.

So, anyway, this is how a career ends. A job that isn't really necessary anymore. Stay-at-home Dad. Once again, many years after being considered a viable candidate, a top prospect, I'm being downsized. Not outsourced, so there's that, but still it's kind of a bummer. Oh, I'll get to answer some questions from time to time, and have my credibility questioned regarding financials and recipes, weather forecasts and baseball teams. Or, as I've told many an employee, is this a kick in the pants? Get out there and do something new. Find a fresh niche and mine it for nuggets of gold.

Not At All Resembling a Rant – October 2021

What do you do with a language that has the words compost, compute, compote, combust, combine, commune and comport, wandering willy-nilly through sentences all at the same time? And along those same lines, don't get me started with comport, report, purport, transport, import, support, deport and carport. My mom and I spend a lot of time on the telephone checking in on each other to make sure that we're each OK in the time of Covid and wonder about such things. You see, we lose words, from time to time. She's 93 and comes by it naturally. It doesn't trouble her much; when she's telling me about someone she used to know back in the day, and suddenly she can't remember the name of the town where they met, or what it was that they did for a living. "Well, I guess that's gone," she says to me, and I tell her not to worry – that I put a pin in it for when she does remember. It happens to everyone.

We keep talking, Mom and I. We muddle through.

"I can't do the newer crossword puzzles," she reflects, "because they have all of those current pop references. Who is L'il Nas X? What is a twerk? And I can't do the old ones because all the words are slipping away." They're not really slipping away, I say with a modicum of frustration for the unfinished Sunday puzzle in my lap. It's our language. It's full of vocabulary that is intended to confound even the most erudite of us. Or rather, them.

No, I don't tell my Mom what "twerk" means. I draw the line right here.

I know what she means. It's a full-time job for some part of our brains to keep all the words in their proper order, filed with the right definitions and usages. Otherwise, we have chaos. And it doesn't help that the pop culture – and by that I mean all of it, from the 24-hour news cycle talking heads to the Instagram meme-creators and propagators – insists on ruining words. Like "fake." Or "efficacy." It's not OK to take a good, simple word like fake and use it so often that it is befouled with the constant context of that usage. Fake smells bad now. It was never fresh to begin with, but today it really stinks. I implore you to put it away, in a Ziploc. Find out what the half-life is for such an odor.

We, Mom and I, each sit in front of an old New York Times puzzle, bound in a large print compendium. I bought two copies and sent one to her. We're mutually baffled by the fact that the editor of this volume chose to leave out the titles of the puzzles – an important tool indicating the direction of some of the clues within. So instead of having a vague idea what "Bronx Five Takes a Little Off the Top," might possibly mean, it's just annoying. Of course, clever often manifests as annoying. And Mom has become fractious in her dotage. I think she misses doing the puzzles with my Dad, who cheated when he worked them with her in the quiet time between after-church and dinner, when he hoped that there was a fresh peach or two left on the kitchen counter ripe enough to cut and eat, mix it with some blueberries in the fridge into a bowl with a little sugar sprinkled on them. Just a bit of fruit compote. Pop would read clues to her having already worked them out – just to make it a team effort, to be able to grin and say "exactly!" while writing in the answer with his pen, to have that time together with Mom sharing something. Of course, she would sometimes get up from her chair and take the puzzle away from him and fill in the boxes of clues he didn't know. He liked the wordplay. Mom, I know now, as her new crossword partner, likes the steadiness of it. Appreciated that there may very well be words that now exist only to be placed into crossword puzzles.

For example, the term "adit." Which means a horizontal passage leading into a mine for the purposes of access or drainage.

I enjoy the games within the puzzles, and often end up with the feeling that our language is just a jumble of syllables that sound similar with no commonality whatsoever but to make the people creating the clues think they're clever. Nevertheless, I experience unbridled joy by unravelling that Bronx Five is not a crosstown highway or a jazz combo but Joe DiMaggio, and taking a little off the top is not illegally skimming funds but a haircut, and so the answer to the clue is "YANKEECLIPPER."

Those of us who still like language, the luxuriousness of words with many, many definitions, who love to expand our vocabulary just to do it, so that we might have pusillanimous at our fingertips or know what a deadly-venomous golden lancehead viper is and where, on an island just off the coast of Brazil, it is the top of the food chain. Well, we are troubled. We're the grammar police. We're insufferable, only they don't use that word, because they don't know that word.

I recently heard someone use the word abscess in the place of the word obsess. I was going to correct them, or at least ask if they meant something different, but I did not. Correcting someone has gone the way of the dodo, like using the term "going the way of the dodo." At the time, they were obsessing about the TV show "The Bachelor," so they may actually have been referring to an abscess, but I'm pretty sure it was just a lingual hiccup. (And I choose to coin that term because I don't know what it is when someone does this – replaces a word with an almost-homonym. Which isn't a thing.)

Lingual hiccup. We all have them. I just discovered, finally, the pronunciation for the word "amalgam," which I kept trying to shoehorn into my vocabulary as ah-mul-gahm instead of the proper uh-MALL-gum. Who cares about my mispronunciation? My friend John, who thinks that the English language is declining like the Roman Empire, only way faster.

Mom and I (in truth, mostly me, but she enjoys my calls anyhow) talked recently about what the person was thinking who named a particular warship a "frigate." Certainly this was a coincidence rather than correlation, nor causal to any sinkings. Oh, frig it anyhow. (See, It's funny! Well, in a dad-joke sort of way.)

And it has been brought to my attention that while homonyms are words that are spelled alike and sound alike but mean two different things - rose the flower and rose up from my seat at the table - Homophones can be spelled alike, too, but don't have to be – rain, rein and reign. My answer to that? Kill me with noxious gas or a chunk of coal.

You know, either ether or ore.

Production – December 2021

When I was very young, my parents bought me a rock tumbler. If you are not familiar with this, it is a device that you fill with pebbles, sand and water and as it rotates the action rubs the sand and water against the pebbles and makes them smooth. If you start out with the right kinds of pebbles, and the right type of sand, with enough polishing you can end up with something quite beautiful. My tumbler came with little packets of sand in different "grits," and excellent instructions for how to successfully polish rocks.

What the kit didn't come with was rocks. This was not a mistake, or an oversight on their part. I imagine that they assumed you had rocks already, or why would you bother to decide to polish them? And nowhere in those excellent instructions was there any assistance with regards to finding rocks. Again, it was implicit that you either already knew or that they imagined it was so elementary a concept that it didn't need further explanation: "Have rocks." Or, also somewhat helpfully: "get rocks."

But in not providing this directive, an important detail was missing. What type of rocks work best in a rock tumbler? I didn't know, and there was no easy way to find out – in this pre-internet world. I gathered some gravel from the gutter by the street in front of my house, because I was in a hurry to get started, to start the process, to hear that tumbler…tumbling.

Adding the packet of grit and the water – both in appropriate measure, to my literal pounds of gray gravel, I tightened down the lid, set it on the rotation mechanism sitting on the desk in my bedroom, checked the pullies for tension, and plugged it in. And the motor hummed, the device turned, and the gravel tumbled in the sandy water.

Loudly. Constantly.

Somehow, my parents let this continue to happen. Although they wanted me to turn it off at night, I insisted that it was necessary for the tumbling to be incessant in order for it to work. OK, they said. Three weeks. Then it must stop.

I didn't tell them what I'd already learned, having read the instructions. That it would be three weeks with the coarsest grit sand, then I would need to rinse everything and start the second stage with the middle-grit sand. Two weeks of that. Then the fine sand, for two more weeks! Yes, best to keep that information to myself. Never light a bridge on fire before you're standing in the middle of it, looking down at the raging water and… crocodiles.

I let the tumbler do its job. I could smell the electric motor heat of it, constantly turning night and day. I fell asleep to the grumbling purr, woke to the crashing ocean wave sound. Then it became the regular background, and I could ignore it.

My friends, on the other hand, were fascinated. Can we open it and look? No. Can we just peek? No. Why not? It will make a mess. We can clean it up? Ha! No. When will it be done. I checked the milkman's courtesy calendar hanging on a tack on my wall. August.

Are you kidding me? No…

You see, I knew what my friends lacked was patience. One had taken apart his magic eight-ball to see how it knew that he was never going to kiss Camille who lived down the street. The other had broken open his older brother's lava lamp because he thought it looked like bubble gum. It did look like bubble gum. It didn't, however, taste like bubble gum. And his brother thumped him pretty hard, which made it all the more disappointing. And I wasn't that much better. I was desperate for Christmas around the middle of October. I couldn't get my Valentine's candy to last until Easter. Who could?

But I let the tumbler tumble, without trying to push it to spin *faster*, or picking it up and shaking it, or cracking it open under cover of Saturday afternoon boredom. And then it was three weeks and I unplugged the motor. One by one, I unscrewed the wingnuts that secured the lid. Peeled the rubber gasket and looked.

Muddy water. Slightly smooth gray stones. I rinsed one in the bathroom sink. Very little improvement. Slightly smooth, *clean* gray stone. I'd hoped for something else. Something…lovely, as a reward for my mighty endurance.

Or a lesson learned. I didn't even have that. When I asked if I could start the second stage of tumbling (I don't know why – the gravel was never going to look like jewelry, like fanciful precious stones in a crown) I was denied. Too noisy. It's done enough. Maybe one of your friends could put it in their bedroom for the second stage. I sulked at the waste of time, my valuable ten-year-old time. I moped at the idea of sharing this project with anyone else, even if it meant moving forward with it. I asked if I could plug it in somewhere else – the basement, the kitchen. The living room! No, no, and no.

I would like to tell you, in a wrapped-up-in-a-bow conclusion that this made me the writer I am today – slightly stoic, able to keep on tumbling day after day, week by week, even when the going gets rough. Or am I finally wise enough to see that if you start with gravel, no amount of polishing is going to make them precious gems. Boy, I wish.

Parting Thoughts… – January 2022

I've been noodling about a piece I'm writing on the end of the world. Perhaps this is because it's been so *en vogue* to speculate about the demise of the species that it's gone full *passe*, or that I want to create the perfect dystopia (because who doesn't?), or that it is just to have fun shooting at lots of bad stuff, like a state fair water-balloon pop, while remaining politically correct - blaze away at zombies all you want, buddy!

I intended to get in my two cents about the world's swan song before no one cares, but I've failed to find traction on or attraction with any bits that had the full complement of truth, whimsy and pathos. In other words, it is not easy being teasy, cheesy and queasy. Maybe no one cares anymore. They're all exhausted with the current reality, which is pretty damned tiring. How often can you be on fire before there is no fuel to burn?

And it's not because I don't care that the world ends. Or that I'm not interested in the details of how our human era of the world wraps itself up. I do and am, inasmuch as such thoughts are integral to the theme of my WIP, and development of the story requires me to come up with an avenue for the possibility of survival, even temporarily. And I have time for such mawkish speculation. Are we doomed? Of course – eventually the atomic pile we call our Sun will come apart at the seams. That's a billion years down the road, mind, and not a front-burner issue (no pun intended). More to the point, what can we do to prevent our doom? Regarding the Sun's end, not very much. Seed the galaxy with our progeny? Common Sci-Fi stuff. Wrestle with God and philosophy and find peace with group-demise? Sure, sure, as my friend John sometimes dismisses the obvious. But one observation keeps popping up in my notes, and plays havoc with my plot arc: can we stop the battle between fools and the less foolish? I don't think we can.

Do you walk around the house barefoot? Of course you do. Why? Because it's your home, and you imagine that you've earned the right to not be encumbered by footwear. Do you ever stub your toe? Of course you do. Do you rage at the gods when it happens as the exquisite pain radiates up your leg to your brain, and toss tomorrow right down the toilet with regards to happy lack of ache in the extremities? You do, admit it. My point (and the larger point about humanity and it's choices) is that you can sometimes prevent calamity, but you choose not to. Or, rather, you choose a different path – one that you walk with no protection for your delicate second toe, the one with no apparent purpose other than finding blunt objects first, and colliding with them. Final question: has this happened more than once – your barefoot dashing of a toe on a chair leg or door left ajar? Really? I'm not judging, just observing.

It intrigues me how different times (and moods) create fresh popular perspectives on the world's end. Viruses – man-made, cosmic, accidentally or intentionally released – were fictional fodder in the nineteen-sixties and -seventies. Zombies, too, found their way into our consciousness around the same time. The ideas nestled into our memory-banks and found root. Each generation of creative types relaunched the sub-genre and we giggled and screamed and clutched our throats anew.

Then reality stepped in, and here we are, wondering *what will happen next?*

My youngest and I were sitting on the porch not so long ago, and she asked me 'what if there were a zombie apocalypse?' I tried to explain without going into much serious detail what I considered possible about such a turn of events.

Selfishly, but only occasionally, I imagine myself in my semi-quiet little corner of the world as it implodes, burns, floats, freezes, chews itself up, spits out the remainder and we happy few still around deal with the too hot, too cold, too dry, too wet, too dead, too undead pieces? Drinking coffee as everything unfolds. And for what it's worth, why are all of the pop apocalypse entries of the last few years so selfish-minded? Do people really want to believe that the world is collapsing under the burden of human misbehavior, and if so, they can actually prepare for or survive it? Or that they can spend their treasure putting together a fool-proof alternative to joining the rest of us in the never-never?

You're right. Please. Enough questions, already.

Cleaning House – February 2022

I'm not very good at letting go of things. Some things. I can easily let go of certain ideas. Others hang on and I have to wheedle the knots out carefully or, like wet sneakers, they will be stuck on me and the shoelaces have to be cut loose. Yes, this happened to me when I was young: Chuck Taylor high tops, worn in the Passaic River while fishing for carp. They were never the same again, and I only got one pair a year, so…

Particular moods stay with me and I have difficulty shaking them. Maybe I think too much. To clarify, maybe I think about whatever I'm thinking about too much. I think about seeing someone, just to talk about what I'm thinking about. The person I think about seeing should be both a therapist and a barista. And we should meet outside, on a bench, like two old secret-agents from the Cold War, going over the past and wondering how it all changed so quickly and completely. Spilling a little spirit from a flask into the coffee, because it's still not Springtime.

I promise – I'm not making fun of therapy. This is just how I feel my therapy should take place. Like a spy-thriller, with mysteries to be revealed, guilt and innocence yet to be determined.

It is sort of funny to me that anger is not one of my moods that linger. Funny strange, not funny ha-ha. But even though I release anger and it dissipates, it still leaves something behind; an odor, scuffs on the floor that don't buff out. Embarrassment, on the other hand, remains as tacky as a newly varnished tabletop. And to belabor this metaphor, it reacts poorly to touching, just to see if it's dry. Fingerprints all over the place, unique reminders of others' impatience with me. Ah, well.

Sometimes I confuse anger with frustration. I can't say why.

They're different, or so I'm assured.

So what is a mood that leaves quickly, and doesn't leave a mark? Accomplishment, for one. Are you also one of those folks who gets something finished, and doesn't get the full satisfaction of having completed the task? I'm not sure why this is how it works for me. One pet theory is that all work is like doing the dishes. Do a good job – no one is impressed. Hurry up and complete the job quickly and there are no kudos, and it doesn't change the truth that you're going to have to do it all over again in a few hours. Take your time, and the same is more or less true. But go ahead and break a dish, and you'll hear about it from everyone, forever.

I have a friend who writes, but never finishes anything – not that I know of, anyhow. In our writing-group, he sits quietly, listens to us offering suggestions, hints and tips about our craft. Or something like that. Occasionally, when we ask, he reveals his works-in-progress early, shows the printed pages, even reads excerpts aloud. We are happy that he is happy with what he has finished so far. We share our pleasure in the pithy dialogue, the textured beginnings of plot development. Then he explains via synopsis what will happen next. And nothing happens next. The papers seem to flutter to the ground like leaves from a tree, awaiting something else, something more momentous. But for my friend, apparently, the harder work isn't fun, and comes with no assurances. So he receives any accolades - his satisfaction - during the process of initial reveal. Whatever he deems sufficient in the writing process arrives in those moments. Why bother to finish a story? What good can come from working more, working harder, only to possibly let down the audience and, therefore, himself? Or to create something good, but no one cares. To do your part, only to have the other half of the boat sink anyway.

Hint: we're all in a boat together. A great big sailboat. You should tell me if there's a leak up in your end of this boat, and I promise to do the same.

It feels vaguely like truth: committing to just enough. Don't do something well – there's no point to it. Being on the receiving end of a lack of support or appreciation…in a word - sucks. I don't know what to call that, feeling (other than suckish?) but I get it and it hangs on like a summer cold. (Or what summer colds used to be before we either didn't acquire them through our masks or were terrified by the sensation of a sore throat and sniffles.) Is our accomplishment's short-lived-ness simply resentment? Or perhaps something more complex? Aren't there lessons, therapies, entire religions dedicated to helping us through the moments of disappointment that come with some assembly required but no clear instructions.

I think mediocrity, half-assed effort, *incompletion*, exist (flourish) because sincerity of effort often runs into the wall of facetiousness, sarcasm, cynicism, drollery, caustic humor and every other behavior substituting for wit. Earnestness cracks beneath the weight of contempt like pottery. No one appreciates effort. They hardly give a good goddamn about results.

And, alas, in this corner of the seventh ring of hell, we have rejection. The blank stare. The blank phone-screen. The short emotional note. The short unemotional note. Swipe left. Spinning in circles with one sneaker nailed to the floor, wondering where oh where I went wrong.

What can I say about being told no that hasn't been hashed over a thousand times in a hundred ways? Do you need me to tell you that there are myriad reasons for "no" beyond the pure dislike of someone or something?

No you don't. I didn't think so…

Low-Magnitude Problems – March 2022

When I was young, I had a problem with nosebleeds. Not from climbing too high in the rafters of a sports arena or taking a left hook in a boxing match, but just *because*. Sometimes from an unforeseen bumping, sometimes an idle finger. Sometimes even spontaneously, sitting at my desk at school, looking at a division problem on the blackboard and suddenly feeling something wet on the back of my hand, looking down and seeing the deep blush of red of what should only be happening with a battle-wound but was just my nose deciding to suddenly drip.

I dwelt somewhere between embarrassing and traumatic, as much as that word is overused. To me it was, anyway. Curious to my friends. Off-putting to my peers. Interruptive to my teachers. If I would have known these words when I was six or seven, I would have positioned myself with a head shake and a "what the fuck?" and embraced each event for what it was: a sideshow. That might have turned disconcerting into cool. But I never had that skill of timing and readiness with a remark. Few of us do.

Instead, I was appalled with myself whenever it happened – in the classroom, outside at recess – because it made people look at me, and that was bad. Not that I didn't want people to look at me. I was pleased to spell words correctly during bees or catch a fly at kickball. I was happy back in the days when my school report card pleased my parents. (Less so later, when it reflected my scholastic…deterioration.) But my shock at…leaking life caused consternation. Nothing good comes from consternation.

Think of a time in your own life when circumstances felt like they gathered to pit themselves against you. Not against your best interests, but rather against you in the moment. Playing happily by yourself or with others – time to sit down on a bench with your head leaning back and somebody's old tissues jammed against your nostrils. *Press hard – to curtail the flow!* Sketching a picture of a SPAD biplane in your composition book instead of doing your reading comprehension test – lean back again, more tissues, and why weren't you doing your schoolwork?

Here's what happened, back in the day, to skinny boys who bleed from time to time. Nothing. Not much of a damn thing. It was not the end of the Romanov dynasty and I didn't hire Rasputin to help me get back into the Class Double-A kickball squad. I wasn't held up to the scorn of the mob, and then scourged, tried and marched up the hill. I didn't die, everyone attended my funeral and wept and gnashed their teeth at the loss of so much potential at such a young age.

Yeah, right.

Occasionally I had to get out of the swimming pool. Sometimes, I couldn't go out and play basketball, or have friends over until it stopped. My mom didn't keep me in a bubble, or stuff a protective helmet down on my head. (Not that parents shouldn't do this, in certain circumstances.) She said, "you'll outgrow this." Which turned out to be true, but I don't know for certain that she actually knew this, or was feeding me a line of bullshit. If she was, it was a very good line of bullshit. My nose did stop bleeding. I stopped feeling like a dork, well, most of the time. And if I did feel like one, I learned to embrace the silliness of actually being one. My daughters will attest to that.

Conclusion? I'm somewhat foolish but not so much so to imagine that this is remotely the same as anything else that many people deal or have dealt with on a regular basis – that is, events that alter how we traverse our planet, that affect our perspective. Negative Issues that happen with such regularity that we tend to ignore them, unless or until they're happening to us.

My situation was not even in the same ballpark. Of course, not everything in the universe needs to be compared – in competition – with everything else. A comment, an observation, a story, can be stand-alone. Even, or perhaps frequently, a character's conflict - human to human, human to nature, human to supreme being – can be low-impact and remain relevant. It is all in the telling of the tale.

And I would say that I was lucky, but I don't believe in luck. There are only truths and perceptions. I didn't know as much as I should about the former and try to hone the self-righteous judgment out of the latter. That's just me, though. As always, your results may vary.

Memory Palace – April 2022

There's a lot of stuff going on, and much of it is not good and often it's hard to find a place for one's brain to be that allows a bit of respite, so forgive me if I reminisce for a little while. Although this is something that I know doesn't help everyone, it is something that works for me. Feel free to place your burdens down, too, if you want.

I occasionally spend time wandering around in the past. My past, anyway. A while back I learned that this pastime, if you will, is called creating a memory palace. A memory palace is a tool called the *method of loci,* an ancient mnemonic strategy considered useful for keeping specific details – people's names, numbers and other things we tend to forget. By visualizing the size, shape, color and location of things, one can recall other items that were, well, just out of reach.

Of course, I may be oversimplifying this, but I do use the concept as I understand it, although not to remember words to a speech I have to make, or where I put my car keys. For me it is rather a way of seeing quite clearly bits from my childhood, the places, people and events, and expanding outwards from them to find more parts of my life-puzzle.

I haven't been back to my hometown in quite a long time. Part of the reason is that there is little that remains there of my childhood. The house I grew up in is a different color, a different shape (more recent owners have made changes) and the proportions are different. There were many large trees on our little ¾ acre. They are gone. Perhaps a storm made them fall, or they were sold for their value as lumber. I don't know. It is just as plausible that big shade trees don't have street appeal anymore. That would be a shame, I think. A big maple tree is an excellent source of calm and summer relaxation.

The old two-rail fences scattered along the street must be a thing of the past, too. They were wearing out when I was young. A kind of yard demarcation status-symbol, they kept nothing in the yard, and no one out. As kids we sat on them, performed high-wire acts of balancing along them, jumped over or crawled through them, chased by dogs, younger or older brothers. Who still owns such a thing? Today we want privacy, intimacy, a place to release the hounds or protect our plots of tomatoes. A yard is not for sharing anymore, unfortunately. The sounds of laughing children annoy us, for some inexplicable reason.

My best friend growing up had a basketball backboard and hoop bolted to the side of his house over the garage. His mother heard us outside, bouncing the ball, many hours through the summer days. The thump of it on the driveway and off the wooden backboard counterpointed everything – Sinatra on the radio, the groan of the Electrolux, the afternoon TV soaps. A small price to pay for knowing where your children (and the neighbors' kids) were.

There's another point to not physically revisiting the past haunts, though. I retain what I consider a clear picture in my mind of my home. No, wait, it's more than that. Pictures and sounds and music and scents and tastes. All of it together in a mélange of recollection, in the memory palace. Unspoiled by change, by storms or changes in taste. I can still start at a point, say the strange, tilted front porch of my childhood home, with the squeaky glider-couch and see through the screen to the dappled front yard. Yes, I know it is bigger in the past than now – because I have grown, aged, and my perception of distance (and time) have altered. A day is no longer a day, so to speak. I can see across to the public library across the street, the parking lot half-full and the empty phone booth near the street.

I can hear the thump-thump of my friend dribbling around the corner of my house. He sees me and pulls a quarter from his trousers pocket and so we begin the journey downtown to the luncheonette which is also a candy store. To get there, we must run the gauntlet of two houses in which reside older boys who don't get along with us. Call them bullies. We did.

This day – the one in my palace - however, is free of conflict. The path to the candy store is a series of dog-legs – left, then right, then left again. It leads past a baseball sandlot, and just beyond the edge of furthest left field an empty shallow pond that is filled during the coldest days of winter so that it freezes and becomes a skating rink. A bit further and a large piece of granite with a bronze plate affixed to it has the names of my town's losses during World Wars One and Two. I would imagine that it is a larger plaque now, so many years later. Behind it is a flagpole, and I can hear the tuneful clang of the brass devices that hold the grommets of the flag overhead.

Look both ways and cross the street. Then cross the train tracks – left to the west, right to the east. That is how I see the world, a left turn takes me out of town into the rural parts, a right turn eventually leads to the city. Straight ahead is the little store with the screen door that slams behind, and a glass case with penny candy. Cinnamon jawbreakers, Jujubes in pasteboard boxes. Wax-wrapped bubble-gum – five pink pieces to a stick with a large color funny, too. A nickel does it. Perfect – some for now, some for later. My friend stands me to some gum, for which I will repay him next time. (I get a dime allowance for emptying the trash at home. It's worth it to my parents – every can in every room must be carried out individually or in pairs – this is pre-Hefty days. If I forget to put the lid on the big can outdoors, breezes lift and carry litter around the yard.)

We whistle on the way home for luck – it would go badly were we to run into our adversaries with our pockets full of sweet loot. I bite off another hunk of Bazooka when we're at the corner of my yard – home free all.

Why don't you like me? – May 2022

Funny, it's easier now. Easier for me to receive a rejection for something I've written and submitted for publication. Easier to be told "no, thank you." Or even just "nope." Post card, email, what have you – no further explanation.

Wow- it's good to get that lie out there in the open so we can pick it apart. Rejection is not fun. But it can be useful. Or maybe not. Or it depends.

We're curious people – writers. We want to know stuff. And then we want to talk about stuff. We want to tell you about it, whatever *it* is. We're driven to do so, for a multitude of reasons. And after we're done doing so, we want to know what you think. And when we're done hearing from you, we want to tell someone else. An ancient but efficient way to do this is to write it all down and send it to someone for the purpose of getting our tale to you. Someone who decides whether or not this will happen - editors and publishers.

Editors are curious people, too. They want to see what you have to say. And an editor is not a critic, in the classic sense. I know it seems otherwise, but they really want to like the things they read. Just like the rest of us. Unlike the rest of us, however, they have to say something after they're done reading.

And so they inform us that the answer to a submission is a happy yes. Or no. Way more often, we are told no.

And herein lies the conundrum. Having been told so we want to know what the editor or publisher thinks about our tale, the one they don't want to publish. No. Come on, because we're curious people, like I said. No. What didn't you like about our story or novel, poem or essay? Let's say, for the sake of argument, that we could really use the input to make changes, corrections, improvements. Wouldn't that be good, a nice thing to do? Better for your karma? Why can't you take the time to tell us? It would make being told "no" ever so much more palatable, yes?

Still, *no*. That just isn't going to happen. Or, if it does, it will be monetized as an author feedback program. And it will teach you next to nothing, because even armed with information about your work, you will still feel hurt and confused after you get back to the process of writing and submitting.

And yet another enigma. Why this love story instead of that? Why her dragon or wizard or alien space pirate and not mine? It can't actually be because you read that one first, can it? Tell them no and pick me!

How you visualize rejection drives how quickly you recover from the wound of disappointment and the possible infection of discouragement, if you will forgive the heavy-handed metaphors. It is one of the non-secrets of publishing that rejection should never be taken personally. How you are told no is not a measure of your talent or skill or dedication to the craft.

I apologize for the irony but cannot say precisely why writing is an "industry" of assumptions and guesses as to what is good, or what good even means. Come to think of it - everything about writing and publishing is anecdotal. Sure, sure, there are algorithms to determine what readers are looking at, what they like, what drives them to click and possibly purchase. Metrics show publishers and editors and agents what interests are trending. But there is also a "you just never know what will be the next big thing" thing about writing.

Each submission you make, I make, is different. Distinctive in the effort expended during creation, in potential value, different in how it makes us feel when we hit send. I think about that old chestnut - you miss 100% of the shots you don't take. This is cutesy, but true. I've been told no a lot. I know the drill: the stages of rejection. Or I think I do…

The sharp slash of disappointment, followed by a period of discouragement. They're not the same thing. Disappointment is thinking something might happen, that a brass ring was within reach and it was always just a matter of effort/timing/luck/your turn/destiny, and then it does not happen. Discouragement, on the other hand, is feeling that you were wrong about something ever happening – wrong from the beginning. Your effort was never going result in success, no matter how excellent you imagined your work – you were thwarted by circumstances outside your control. It was never going to be your turn – that was just crazy thinking. Why bother sitting down and getting back to work?

Nest – giving and/or getting the kick in the seat of your pants, either by yourself (yes, that seems physically impossible) or by someone else, whose opinion you trust. Where you brush yourself off and sit back down, pen in hand, and start to create again.

Finally, finding the energy to keep going.

I've heard of something called "manifesting" – keeping a positive attitude throughout the work you do, and willing a thing to happen. This doesn't relieve a writer from doing the actual hard work - the creating, crafting and polishing - but it keeps you going, because you have a certain kind of hope, the one that comes from confidence that you will accomplish…something.

Hope is a big part of writing, I think.

Apathetic – Antithetical – June 2022

I step outside on the porch. It is nicer here, now that we are fully within the confines of the vernal equinox, but not yet succumbing to the full-on broil of summer. I prefer it out here, however, regardless of season. Inside is the place of information, and much of that information is…ungood.

Did I hear what happened today? What she said? What they did? Hang on, look at this…isn't it awful? Do you believe it? What is wrong with…

I try to not pay too much attention to things that are ungood. I'm not hiding. I'm not ignoring. I'm just not surrendering everything.

And while that may seem to say that I'm apathetic about what is going on around me - around the world - nothing like this was implied. What I mean – what I am saying – is that I try to not give anything more of my time than is necessary. I don't pay *too* much attention. Just what I consider the correct amount. I feel that giving the ungood more of my focus is impactful on my work, my mood, and my health.

At this point it might be considered by some to be helpful to begin a sentence with "This is not to say I don't think that there are many terrible things going on and I'm appalled by them." But I don't think that repeating something in a new way or taking the same stance from a different angle is peculiarly helpful. Truth? I find it antithetical to repeat thoughts that were clearly stated.

Which may or may not make my point.

Wow. It is difficult to maintain this rhetorical point of view. In the hopes of ostensibly finding common ground, most of us are used to repeating ourselves. Louder, slower, wrapped in our reasoning and context, illustrated with personal anecdotes and lots of synonyms. Increasing the noise, not because we like to hear ourselves, but because we want you to hear us, acknowledge us and come over to our way of thinking. Which is not, by the way, common ground. And so are we frustrated by our own logic, or lack thereof. We're all in this together, we say, we think - craving some manner of confirmation, so that we feel like we're mutually involved. And we want that participation trophy.

Meanwhile, that which we might be doing to some end, the thing we're *good at*, goes by the wayside. Accomplishment, with all of its value, including satisfaction, delayed or just plain gone. In the interest of passive absorption of…everything, we neglect our call, our calling. Do this long enough and we no longer know what that calling is, or how to perform the actions necessary. Our information overload comes with a price, a weight, a tarry stickiness that most of us haven't the energy or disposition to carry forever nor with which to relieve ourselves.

Frost once wrote about the road not taken. How it made a difference for him, to have reached a fork and made a decision one direction over another. I don't think he could have imagined that we would be here, letting lack of choice make us. That we would prefer not to be on the road at all.

Which is why I go out on the porch, with a cup of coffee or tea, with a book, without my phone or laptop. Yes, I want to be aware, but I don't need to have every gory detail precisely when it happens. No one is grading me on my promptness. I want to be productive, too, and sometimes that means recharging, finding the mental energy, the clarity of ideas. I would like to be helpful, if I can be, and as sympathetic and positive as I am able. In an information situation as intentionally shocking as a firehose of cold water, this can only be accomplished with counter-intention on my part. Did I hear? No. Hang on, check this out…. No, thank you. No, it isn't easy for me, either, but I get better with practice.

I turn away from the noise. I turn a corner. I take a deep breath and turn the page.

Why write if no one reads what you're writing? – July 2022

This particular question recently crossed my radar on social media, and nagged at me a little bit. Firstly, because I think I misunderstood the direction of the question. I thought they meant "if I never get published, and therefore don't have a *readership*." But it turned out after some investigation that they literally meant no one. Not one reader, ever – not a friend who is interested in the things you do, no family member who peeks over your shoulder while you're typing, no significant other who wonders what happens to you after dinner when you're at the computer. No one.

And that made me both sad on the one hand, and quite certain that this is the wrong question on the other. The correct wording should be "for whom are you writing?" because if you think no one is reading, well, think again. Who is your audience? Not, "who do you want your audience to be?" or, "how can I / why can't I sell more books?" Those questions are fun, all-consuming in our thoughts, but they are not part of the existential angst that we bring on ourselves in the act of writing.

You are your first audience, your first reader. You're the alpha reader. You have to be the reason you write; your enjoyment of the tale, the verse, the connection between people, the places you have or haven't been. And I feel like further explanation for this conclusion is both necessary and pointless. Unless you're Jack Nicholson typing *all work and no play* in an empty hotel in the dead of winter, then of course you're reading what you write. You are judging your work. You are enjoying the telling and the tale, and you have the unique luxury of being able to fix the things you don't like (or at least mark them immediately for later).

We need to have a personal reason for scribbling (or so I believe) and it ought to be (in my opinion) because we enjoy reading. Love writing because you love reading. Appreciate it. Stick to it. Improve it, by reading. Reading almost everything, consuming words like all the meals we ever imagined, bad and good. And then read our own work and see if the flavors you create are something in that…palette. Hopefully, something we like, but if it's something we don't like, then we're ready to make progress.

If it is hateful, miserable, boring to do this, well…there are a myriad of things to do to fix those moods, including reading more of those things you enjoy. So pull over into those lanes and have more fun at this. After all, it's a game. It's just a game.

There are a plethora of aphorisms I could plug in here, but you've heard them all before, and they aren't always helpful to repeat. Be gracious when you hear them from someone other than me, though. Your people mean well. And I'm not your cheerleader, your critic nor your coach. I'm just another slob out here – typing, typing. I don't really know any more than you already do, and I have no more good sense than you, because I, too, picked up a pencil and started to look for a piece of paper to tell a story, once upon a time. For good or bad.

Neither A Critic Nor An Editor Be… - August 2022

I spend my time reading others' writing. This is a joy. For me, that is. I suspect that it isn't always a moment of confident pleasure for writers to submit their work to be considered for publication somewhere. There are many expectations to be met, on both sides. The writer, for example, has an idea of what it takes to be a contributor; what they bring to the table, the time and effort and skill/talent/inspiration that is required to create, and they release their work accordingly out into the world as something more than just words in the right order. An editor has, or should have, a not-so-secret list of guidelines that meet what they are looking for in a submission, a time allotted to the task – yes, task – of reading submissions, and preconceived notions of quality. This list is often, at least to the writer, something between a map with no coordinates and a Gordian knot, not fun for anyone to analyze, unravel or defuse. To the editor, however, it is a fairly clear picture in their mind of what their journal looks and feels like, and how an accepted submission should fall into that picture easily, like a carefully carved wooden peg sliding in a similarly shaped hole.

There is fine reward when everything comes together. Publication. Pain of many and various sorts when it doesn't. Rejection is hard enough. Making of it a line in the sand is worse.

The process and all of its wishful thinking on the part of both parties leaves much room for conflict, of course, a sort of cold wariness between authors and editors. How to please those… ediots at literary magazines? What don't they see in my 1600 well-crafted words? Or, on the other contentious hand, a brand-new way to show dialogue between characters? What can you actually be thinking? I cannot figure out this POV, so how can my readers? Please give me something new and tasty using off-the-shelf ingredients.

Yeah.

Add to this all of the real restrictions on word quantity (not word length, for crying out loud - feel free to use longer words, unless you think the editor suffers from *Hippopotomonstrosesquippedaliophobia*,) subject matter, triggers, style prompts, what was recently published, what has already been accepted and committed, and language. As in foul, or any other so-called inappropriateness. And the general contentiousness of anything that requires judgment. The idea that we are in competition with each other in everything we undertake.

I think that writers and editors spar with each other, in very slow motion and at a safe (?) distance. And thank goodness, too. If they were in the same room, it would be trouble right here in River City. They think they don't get along with one another. Editors think writers are the problem with writing and writers think editors shouldn't exist, because they…get in the way. So, what can be done about the technicalities of a one-way system? Isn't it a one-way system? Is the power of the publication process entirely in the hands of the publication?

I'm not sure anymore.

Carefully reminding ourselves that editors are allowed to run their publications how they see fit, and that writers are necessary to provide "content" (a word no one likes, I know) for said publications, one would think that this symbiotic relationship would be more amenable. That we could remove the concept of "power" altogether from the so -called equation. Social media (a misnomer, I feel) shows this to not be so, and hasn't helped clarify anything. The writer is a petulant diva working in a vacuum. The editor is an out of touch critic of art with no skills to speak of. The rife tribalism of confirmation bias that the screaming platforms foments fans the flames of publishing culture-wars. Some would say *as well it should.* If there needs to be a revolution, the person once said, let it begin here. But…

My older daughter says that I need to stop doing that. Making an argument beginning with the word "but." That little word implies that I have the floor (I guess I do) and that anyone is interested in my point (are you? Perhaps. Perhaps not.) I may, but who cares? We live in a world where people like me have had their say for so long that we might actually have answers to problems, but no one is listening. They are exhausted with the ancien regime. We've lost our right to belabor the world with our opinions. I get it, I really do. Which still doesn't matter.

So what is left to say? ¡*Viva la revolucion!*

It isn't easy being me – September 2022

I don't know why. I think I'm a terrible listener. I want to talk so very much. Maybe too much. Not always about me, but about…oh, everything.

It's a habit, probably a bad one.

Still, people tell me things. Firstly, they ask questions: have I ever…? Do I know about…? Remember when…? Then they reveal themselves to me: dirty laundry, scars in strange private places, hell, even open wounds.

I tell them I'm a writer (I suppose I am, after all) and I tell them I'm an editor of a literary magazine (it is, after all). And they nod and smile and continue telling me stories. True stories, mostly, as much as they remember them. Or ideas for fictional tales that they haven't put to paper, yet.

And I listen, and ask my own questions, and find myself fascinated and maybe that's why they think I'm a good listener.

My questions almost always begin with "you know you should write this story down, right?" And then I follow with "It's a hell of a thing" or something to that effect, because that's the best compliment I can think of for someone who has a great story in them and hasn't yet written it down. It is a hell of a thing, like having a thorn in your foot or a hangover from a great party. Something that needs to be handled. Removed, possibly. And I don't ask too many questions, because to some extent it might be rude. What color was her hair? Probably OK, although I still wouldn't ask because it doesn't really matter. I have a picture of just about everything in my mind's eye, ready to be taken out and used in the movies my brain creates. I would give you better examples, but I cannot. And you will understand why, I hope, by the end of this little essay.

Here's what I don't say: I can help you write your story if you want me to. I never say it. It's rude, I think.

I've thought about this a lot – the unspoken question, the offer never voiced. I do want to help. Almost desperately. Almost but not quite. And, as they say, therein lies the difference. Because they're not my stories. Not mine. I'll be honest with you. Right now there are six very, very good yarns in my head; things told to me over coffee, or sitting on a bench waiting for a child's after-school playdate to finish, or during dinner or some other non-event. And if I were so inclined, I could scribble them down. Figure out the fine details as I go. Polish them. Make them quite something. But they're not mine. It would be wrong.

Not that I was held to some sort of blood-oath to not touch the stories. Or, conversely but not equally to the point, the story-tellers themselves are probably never going to do anything with them, in spite of their brief enthusiasm for the craft of writing. Once upon a time, so to speak. But neither of these facts is relevant to me.

Rather, it's that there must be some kind of trust, a particular kind of honor among thieves. Writers are thieves, after all. We do kiss and tell on ourselves, and include others in the story, stealing their personas whether or not they want to be included. For what is a story without characters that remind us of us? Even the Gospels aren't just about Jesus. They're about the other folks, too. Fishermen. Little old ladies. Tax collectors. We don't have them sign release forms, either – we just sweep them up into the narrative. We steal style from those we admire. We steal words – one or two, mind – not a whole bunch of sentences (that would be deeply wrong in our book of rules) – that work where we want them to work. We steal pictures turned into words: places we've been, gardens we've sat in, buses we've ridden on, what have you. No one claims copyright over a flower arrangement. (I don't think. Maybe they do. I guess it's possible.)

But someone else's yarn? Something so interestingly twisted and turned that I cannot successfully extricate myself from the moment, that half-hour across a table where I first heard the tale, asking for a refill of my wineglass and reaching for another handful of pistachios (trust me, they go together), and leaning back to hear the denouement revealed. I know where I was and what I heard, and the sound of the voice telling me what I heard, and how I felt about what I heard. I know that you're not supposed to take that idea, even the kernel of it, and use it.

Wait a minute. Let me rephrase that. I know that *I'm* not supposed to. Maybe it's just me. You make your own decisions.

All that said, there is part of me that wants reach out, to touch base and, somehow – I don't know how – bring up the subjects of those long-ago told tales and try and nudge them along again. *Hey, remember that great thing you told me about? What's up with that? You making any headway with it? No? Really?*

Damn.

Bad on so many levels.

So what happens now? The stories remain in a neatly wrapped bundle on the slushpile of my mind, I guess.

Notes on a life – October 2022

A friend of mine died. It was back in March, but I didn't know, because I was consumed with the health problems of another friend, and I had just emailed him and although I knew that his heart was failing I didn't know that it was not going to last much longer. Perhaps I should have sensed something was happening, something was wrong. He asked me for my home address, said he wanted to send me something, but didn't say what it was. Maybe a picture. Maybe a book. And though I'd given my new addy to him before, I didn't think anything of this re-request. We sometimes ask for something more than once and are chided for not remembering. I don't know what happened to it, he might have typed. No big deal, I would have responded to such a thing. Here you go. Even only typing, without the reassurance of hearing someone's voice, conversations with old friends can be indolent and comfortable, like telling a story to someone who's heard it a hundred times before when you enjoy your own words and they just don't mind that you're doing it again, or maybe they do, just a little, but they cut you that break. That is how friendship works.

He was an artist. He worked in paint, clay, pencils and pens. The world is full of people who can take what they see and make something else out of that vision, raw or refined, complex or spare. I am not one of those people. I don't resent the lack, but I respect that capacity in those souls I come across. I'm sure you know what I mean; you know someone who can draw or carve or dance or sing or build or compose. Don't you like knowing them? Isn't it special? I think it is.

He didn't follow many rules. Had a tough time with certain kinds of authority. Colored outside the lines, sometimes. Didn't believe in God, except in that he saw all of nature – creation - as something remarkable, fantastic. The creation out there. That which came from inside himself, and others. All divine.

He had a big heart. His morality was a simple one that requested we all be nice and share. A child's idea of right and wrong. He gave things away – anything he had, things he made and things he found that he thought you might like or need. Sometimes he came over and needed to sit in the woods and work or just to get some peace and quiet - asked me for a folding chair and did I have any beer in the fridge? or where was my fishing gear? Such simple audacity made it easy to tell him yes and *over there* and make himself at home. I wished I could be like that, all of the time. I still do.

He made a life-sized clay bust of me one Saturday, long ago. Before the hurricane, as I track things. When there were so many more tall old trees in the woods. I sat in my kitchen, and he spread everything out on the table: an oilcloth tarp and the plywood plank upon which he had affixed an armature and a burlap sack of brown clay. The armature was a small white skull, troublingly realistic. He talked while he warmed the clay in his hands and began attaching it, bit by deliberate bit, to the armature. About work, which he was about to quit, because he was planning to relocate. About his family and their crazy lives. He knew people, vaguely famous people in art and in music and in that way that someone who is gregarious and odd and interesting is permitted to infiltrate themselves into the world of celebrity. He would tell me when it was OK to take a sip of coffee and when I wasn't allowed to move around, so I mostly had to watch him work out of the corner of my eye. The memory, therefore, is more auditory and peripheral than I wish it was. Don't we all have moments in our lives that we wish were more intentional, more aware of their importance down the long road?

Not long after that – when the clay bust was sitting, slowly drying before firing in a studio the next town over, he did leave, went north to a city where he'd found an old house he could afford – one of those situations where both house and city need so much work that no one even considers them fixable. He got it for a song and started in on it – tearing our walls and re-glazing windowpanes. I've taken out all of the bedrooms upstairs, he told me and turned it into one large loft. Lots of light for painting. Or a basketball court. I wouldn't have been surprised if he wasn't joking. He found work to do that paid enough and grew his own vegetables in the little front yard – if you're going to grow food, you should be ready for people take some, so make it easy for them – and drew and painted.

He didn't pass away. And by that, I mean that I think passing away is for people worried about dying. I could be wrong. I often am, about death. But Jim didn't worry about it. Didn't run full speed towards it, either. He just wasn't all that upset that his health hadn't been great for a while, that of all things it was his heart that gave him trouble. He missed working, told me that sometimes he was just bouncing off the walls bored, but that wasn't very often. There was a fairly long period when what he did, volunteering on a suicide hotline, kept him out of his paints and pencils. He said, without complaining, that it drained his creative energy, and yet he gave it freely away. I asked myself more than once, who does that? Who makes that sort of sacrifice?

Near the end, he was back to drawing, because he could hold and control the pencils, but not painting, because brushes didn't quite go where he wanted them to. He didn't mind, though. Or, perhaps he did, but he kept that to himself, too.

Pop Culture Denial – November 2022

It's a thing. Occasionally I've heard a friend or family member claim not to know anything about Tik Tok or who Ed Sheeran is. Or the Kardashians. What is "wordle?" Or Venmo. Or an NFT.

Oh, come on, you know! Someone will say. (Me, for example.)

Nope.

And not just current popstuff, either. Someone who states they've never listened to the Rolling Stones, or heard of much less read Rolling Stone Magazine, or never follow/ever followed Saturday Night Live or know what you mean when you say, "Here's looking at you, kid."

No. Way. It's from Casablanca. The movie.

I never saw that, the response, which is remotely possible, but still just doesn't work, I say, because Bogie has climbed out of the confines of celluloid and leached into every aspect of Western Civilization. The Rolling Stones play each building in every elevator. OK, maybe not Mick and the boys, but calm, quiet cover-doppelgangers. Right?

So I am trying to figure out this thing, this behavior, of being unaware of the unavoidable. Intentional ignorance. So that they, what? Seem more cultured? By pretending that you spend time buried underneath a rock you are somehow smarter – how does that work? Are they just picking an argument?

Or am I ignorance shaming? Not sure that's a thing.

Maybe they prefer not to clog their circuits with the burnt and melted marshmallow of the fifteen-minutes famous. I mean, if you miss one influencer as they pass, don't worry – another will be along soon. Waiting to read a book until time has supposedly validated its worthiness is…something. A measurement of some ilk.

I'm going to turn this on myself. To wit: it has been difficult of late staying on top of the mélange that is socio-political diatribe and social-media rage. I do my best...

Sorry, that's a big old whopper. I don't even try anymore. That makes me…what? A newsless wonder? Out of touch? I cannot answer the question "Did you see…?" without seeming dim, lacking a clue. For I did not see.

And it isn't just keeping up with the nightly/daily/every eighteen minutes newscycle. Do I stream TV shows? Some. None of them have singers, masks or judges. Do I watch superhero movies? Some. None of them have singers or judges. Can I explain NFTs? Not well, but passably. And I have read all I want to know about crypto-currency and have found myself not wanting.

And I understand, just now, right this moment, that there isn't an iota of difference between those people who can't spell Lady Gaga, much less pick her out of a lineup, and me. One person's not giving a damn about Britney is another's tired headache for the crumbling of the republic.

Maybe there are more ways than one of looking at this. You can decide for Oxford commas, just to rock the boat. (The damned sentences work, regardless of that extra little tittle. Let it go.) You can be overwhelmed by choices, like paper checks, online banking, PayPal and Venmo. (I swear, I don't know how that last one works any more than I can explain the inner workings of an automatic transmission. If I had some time, I would just drive it – so to speak - and become one of its advocates, comfortable in my lack of knowledge accompanied with practical experience. In the meantime, don't get behind me in the grocery store checkout.)

And here's a brief conclusion I've reached. It's about what we do to each other. How we treat one another. We say, "you don't know what you're talking about." We say, "I don't know what you're talking about." They're not the same thing at all, but each claim puts the onus of ignorance on the other person. That you don't know what they meant, or why they said what they said, or what in the living hell they meant by what they said. Or why they said anything at all.

How about we give this alternative a try: watch what you want to watch, read what you want to read, wear what you want to wear, dance how you want to dance, take pictures of your food, your dog, your dog's food. Follow what you want to follow. Share. Be nice.

Something on my mind… - December 2022

We – that ubiquitous pronoun that supposedly means more than one but otherwise reveals so little – are parting ways one with another. And not just petulantly saying goodbye, ghosting in whatever way the words or actions manifest themselves, but moving socially, spiritually, politically, morally, tribally, physically, and chronologically apart.

Like tectonic plates inexorably shifting, only way, *way* faster.

There's a great deal to this, but at least part of the…current *differentiation* between us has to do with our vocabulary. When we use our words – as our parents used to entreat us to do when we were mere ankle-biters – we have an expectation that others within hearing distance understand what we're saying. There is an assumption that those others speak the same language as us. This is not always the case, of course, and we resort to frustrated and even angry increase in volume and frequency, tone and repetition, in the hopes that we can be understood. When we are not understood we become desperate in our disparateness.

Louder, slower, more frustrated. Repeating aloud the same thing, again, hoping for some new result. Becoming angry at others, at ourselves, when that new result doesn't manifest. Acting out our anger. These are not the actions of a society, however we choose to define that word.

Why aren't we on the same page? We're speaking the same language, aren't we? No. And I don't mean the words brought into this society by other cultures, introduced additions to our vocabulary that enhance, advance and nourish the variety of our lexicon.

I mean the acronyms, shorthand or slang terminology that are created by every generation, with the intention of setting generations apart. Those may be a necessary aspect of life. A minor fad-cryptology, if you will, that permits kids to irk their elders. Fire, sick, righteous, cool, bitchin', wizard, keen, neat-o, swift.

Or *twenty-three skidoo*.

T'was always thus, I am told. But it seems very poor timing of late. Purposefully engage in the parting of ourselves, into us'es and them's, smaller and smaller subsets, the sense as well as the reality of a "we" in society is that we are becoming tinier dots on the communication Venn diagram, without, I suspect, even thinking about it. Certainly not considering some of the consequences. In our efforts to find something to belong to – most of us want to belong – we are creating fences that separate us. Sharp, splintery things.

But fences make good neighbors! goes the old chestnut. Fences keep things in. And out. They protect, but they divide. Fences permit privacy, but they hide. Good and bad, help- and harmful.

And, if we keep sorting and classifying ourselves into ever reductive subsets, "we' will inevitably become "me." Me, compartmentalized and alone. Me doing what I want, when I want. Me saying things without regards for anyone else, not caring, not aware. Me not worried at all about not comprehending what that person over there is saying, much less thinking how we are related. Seeing no consequences at finding no common ground.

Or I could be wrong. Maybe how we use our words is not as big an issue as I think. Maybe we're good at being both tribal and a larger thing, a society. Maybe. I doubt it, though.

Twenty-three skidoo. Do you know what I mean? Has that term ever crossed your radar? Not so very long ago, it was just a bit of silliness painted on the door of a Ford roadster jalopy. Did it ever actually mean anything?

Funny how origins get muddy. Saying this, the following may or may not be accurate. What I've read is that supposedly, the faddish saying of "twenty-three" originated in the first showing of an 1899 play made from Dickens' "A Tale of Two Cities," in which the main character, Sidney Carton – going to the guillotine in place of someone else – is being beheaded "by the numbers." Sidney steps up, gives his number – twenty-three – and that's that. Edgy, hip folks of the gilded age found that…interesting enough to start throwing "twenty-three" into conversation. Interrupt me? Twenty-three, pal. Want to dance? Twenty-three, darling. How are you doing? Twenty-three!

And we think that skidoo comes from *skedaddle*, a slang term that was being said, shouted even, as far back as the American Civil War when troops saw the other side running away – Look at them blue-bellies skedaddle! - or when they entreated each other to do the same. A bit of British slang - "scaddle" - precedes that, pointing backwards to the Irish (gaelic) word for scatter - "sgedadol." Now we have a code term that means what we want it to mean, at any given moment – Time to go, baby. Drop whatever you're doing. Let's leave, your father is a real jerk, isn't he? Twenty-three skidoo!

What is the point? Why not just say scatter? Because *we* don't want *you* to understand what we just said. It isn't *for* you.

Left, right, red, blue, fake, real, great, hate, cancel, believe, think, know, truth.

"Inspo" – January 2023

I don't know about you, but when certain things happen, I am intrigued and want to know more about them. Like "inspiration dreams." Why do they happen to me, and how can I get them to happen more often? Am I doing something special? Do they happen to others? Am I depending on them to get over inertia. Is it possible I'm *misdefining* inertia? So many questions…

An inspiration dream, for a writer, is that slightly fantastic moment when you aren't sure – can't really believe – that something so wonderful and clear and *competent* has happened during your sleep that you should get out of bed and go and scribble down as quickly as possible what you just experienced. Sure, you're tired and a bit addled. Sure, sure, it is also possible that this will actually make sense, be something, in the morning when you look at it again, however the only writing implement close to hand is a pink highlighter, so there will be a fair bit of decryption involved. *Stay down*, says your internal Mickey to your Rocky. You've been knocked around too many times. *Watch that bum eye, kid.*

Here's what it's like to have a complete, or seemingly nearly so, work-in-progress pop into your skull: exhilarating, frustrating, furiously curious and enlightening. All at once. Like a Long Island Ice-Tea, if you know what I mean. The bartender doesn't care how many you consume. Pace yourself and tip your waitress. What could possibly go wrong?

Like you, I'm often tired at night, when I'm in bed. I get up anyway. Wander carefully downstairs to my office, where the computer waits in silent readiness. Try to not stub my toe on the full laundry basket parked in the dark hallway like Sam Spade with his gat in hand. Illuminated in the pale blue light of the screen I begin typing, trying to recapture as much of the dream feed as possible – character descriptions, scene mood, plot devices, time-and-place. Any punchlines to jokes, just in case they were actually new and funny.

When I think I have it all – I never have it all – I pad back up to bed.

Don't settle for jotting down keywords. You will wake up to jibberish. Misspelled jibberish, which is worse. Instead, write what you saw. Where did it happen? Who was there and what they looked like.

Dialogue is key, as we all know. I try and recapture any dialogue I can. What were people saying and why were they saying it? If it's done correctly, dialogue between characters moves the plot along, maintains pacing. In most dreams, of course, it is gobbledegook. A sci-fi fantasy with dragons fighting Martians turns into your sophomore year Geometry teacher asking you why you don't know side-side-angle-side. Or is it sine, sine, cosine, sine? I don't know. This is a terrific way to determine if you're down a rabbit hole. Or a sign-sign you're even cogent, sigh.

Go back to bed when you find that you've forgotten more than you remember. I find that dreams are like that, ephemeral, flighty, mysterious. Don't forget to save your document, for god's sake. Somewhere you can find it again. No, not in the old tax documents. Yes, in your porn stash. Whatever.

Set your expectations low, early and often; that's my advice. You're a writer and you know as well as I do that the very word that describes us should be a reverse-homonym. We are, mostly, wrongers. Entire pages of programming code exist to keep us from poor spelling. Editors exist – or at least used to – to fix our shit.

Writing is the baseball of art forms, where hitting the ball at all, even foul, counts for…something. It isn't all rewarded, either – just like a long drive that curves into the third-baseline seats. Just a groan is all you get, sometimes.

So get up. Grab your reading glasses. And put your slippers on, I beg you.

Job Search – February 2023

I ran into a wall in 2022. Not literally, although that is not beyond me, I am sure. The wall I hit was one of perception. Revelation.

I'm not a "stay at home dad" anymore.

What do I mean? Well, I'm reasonably sure that you know what an SAHD is. When parents make a joint decision that one will work (go to the job function site) and the other will remain home and care for the children during the workday. I apologize if you already know all this, or if you think that me explaining it is a kind of -ism, but when I began doing it, nearly 20 years ago, it was novel, and I was alone on the playground with my girls and their friends and their friends' moms. And at birthday parties. And at the library, or the waiting line after school. It was... amazing. Not the being *alone*, because I wasn't, of course, but the being *there*, for every moment. Making meals, doing chores, helping with lessons, playing, learning with them everything they learned, being asked questions, making memories.

Pretty schmaltzy stuff, I know. Also pretty great. I highly recommend it if you have the opportunity. Even the strange bit at the end, where the pandemic muddled the crisp lines between home, work and school, and occasionally required creative stay-at-home caregiver tag-teaming. Still, getting to be the primary home-parent has been pretty rewarding for me. I learned a lot, raising two girls.

And now they're out, doing their own things. And I stay home. It's quieter. When I wash dishes, I crank up the tunes – the ones I used to dance with the girls to, while we made peanut-butter saltines. We talk on the phone – a lot. About new things, like how college classes are, or what went on today at work. I listen a lot more. They teach me. And we laugh a lot, and remember things that happened when they were little, not so long ago.

What does it all mean? I hit that wall, dusted myself off, got up again. Now what?

Well, things will never be the same. That's good and bad. I liked being Dad. And now being Dad means something new. I still get asked questions, but those questions are…curious. Like "Hey, what happens if I do this?" Not "may I do this?" I have to remember to use my words. Words such as "in my opinion," or "I've always found that…" They must make their own ways in the world, not necessarily my way. And I also have learned that sometimes they just want to talk, not get advice. They don't mind if I ask if this is the case, either.

The days seem longer. I have to fill hours on my own. I am thinking about taking a class. I don't know what in, yet. And when spring comes, I will get a fishing license. Yes, that is cliché. That doesn't make it less of a good idea. The baseball season will return, eventually, and I want a seat in the stands behind home plate, where I won't get too sunburnt, and can read between innings.

When I started out in this stay-at-home-Dad role, my desk was in the living room, in the middle of things. I did my reading and writing after chores or during naps, then during school, and finally late at night when everyone else was asleep. Now, my office, with the books and computer and comfortable chair, is more of a hideaway - with some houseplants I care for and a ticking clock and pictures on the wall and a cup of coffee going cold. It takes a little longer for me to find my groove and be productive, and I can stay on task a bit longer without interruptions. It is as rewarding as ever.

Yet, I miss the interruptions. The sound of cartoons on the television. Swinging on the swings. The call to come draw with me or to play knights-and-castles. The homework check-up. Snack-time.

Man, you can't beat snack-time.

"Umarell" - March 2023

Quick definition – *Umarell* is a bit of regional Italian idiom that refers to men of a certain age who stand around, usually at construction sites, observing the goings on and occasionally commenting to anyone within hearing what they think about the work's progress. Giving unsolicited advice. It is a funny sort of a thing because I doubt there are any of us who cannot see in our mind's eye someone like that. Serious-faced, a grandpa type, hands clasped behind their back, grumbling about the lack of this or that, or too much of something going on. Hard not to smile at such a picture, even more difficult not to see ourselves (yes, you too,) in their place at some time. Soon. Maybe now. What I cannot tell in reading the definition of the idiom is if it is tongue in cheek or a serious thing. Are the men being made fun of?

A while back, Dad wrote a short essay, maybe for an adult Sunday school class he was leading, I don't know, about those things we carry in our pockets, and what happens when we no longer need them. The car keys, some spare change, your wallet. Cell phone. Maybe a cylinder of Life-Savers. A penknife. Clean, folded handkerchief. We stop placing them on our person when there is no longer a purpose. No more car keys. No cash or credit cards, no drivers' license. At some point in our life, perhaps sooner than we want, or later than we imagined, we will have nothing to do with taking care of ourselves. And the bitter truth is that this moment will come upon us, will only happen if we are lucky. If we are privileged to have circumstances where we can afford for a level of care that includes…everything. Like royalty, we will walk around with our hands clasped behind our back, possibly literally, perhaps only metaphorically.

Nevertheless, without our self-worth, our obvious purpose – as represented somewhat by our pockets full of stuff, we begin to feel less ourselves. Less involved. Less useful. Less independent. We rely on our perception of those things to be part of the world we live in. Often we receive our perception as interpretation of how others see us. The obvious devolves into the oblivious. (Yes, that is just me being fatuous with wordplay.)

And so we fade away. Or just fade.

Clasping our empty hands behind our backs because we're done with our pockets. Our pockets. Our apparently empty pockets. That lack is what we fear. Lack of usefulness, lack of value. But there is, not to be cartoonish about it, something out there. We have a perception-glitch that prevents us seeing beyond the horizon, as if it is death and we are not permitted to know until we get there, so to speak.

To me, it is a strange irony (like quarks, ironies come in different flavors – hidden, mad, charming, strange, top shelf, and bottom feeding) that we crave solitude, but not when we don't want it. Unwelcome isolation is simply loneliness, and this is a completely different emotional beast. While solitude may rebuild and restore, loneliness seems to only inflict damage. And, again if we are lucky, we wander our mortal coil making social choices – to be with others or not to be with them (no Danish pun intended), or having those choices made for us. We measure ourselves by what we do, what we accomplish and as the list shrinks, so do we.

May I suggest an alternative plan? Don't surrender. Don't let your usefulness be conditional. Get out there by yourself. Tilt at the windmill confidently, *look, no hands!* Maybe a bit of alone-time, in whatever manifestation that takes, when we've had too much group-think. Or immersion in the crowd, when we feel sorry or sad, to help us get past the moment. Yes, I'm painting with a very fat brush – nothing is ever this simple. But I think the point is valid. Be prepared for loneliness. March forward into it. Tuck your hands into the small of your back and stand outside, observing, nodding, gesturing at the world.

Difference – June 2023

We are different. We have differences. So what?

I think about this. Probably more of late because differences of all sizes and sorts seem to be the center of most conversations.

I am different from you, my elder daughter tells me, over coffee. We sit outside in the spring sunshine. She is working on a freelance project, and I am just sitting in the sun. I have my books with me, but it is nice just sitting here, listening when she feels like talking.

She has determined this difference between us at a young age – she just turned twenty-four. It took me much longer than that to realize how much like my own parents I am. I always assumed that sameness was something to avoid. She, wisely, has measured *same* and *different* and found them not to be exclusive positions.

It's privilege she sees clearly, and explains it to me. She admits that there was a certain type of privilege to growing up the child of a stay-at-home dad. One that reads and writes and likes cartoons going to the zoo and playing in the park and fishing and many other childish things. That she is different from me, is only one point she is trying to make. She is also different from many of her…well they can't be peers, per se, can they? Contemporaries? Yes, let's go with that for now.

Her privilege, she explains, is that she has always been listened to, by her mother and me. Her thoughts have always had merit, her considerations consistently worthy of moments of focus. And, she tells me, this is not normal.

I ask her if this is a good thing. To be different. To be privileged in this manner.

Most of the time, she says, answering the first point – different from me, and then amends her claim. No, probably all of the time, answering the second (more important?) point – how different and fortunate she is from those like her, as she witnesses the…demographic.

Did you enjoy growing up? I want to ask but don't, because if she sees this question coming she will wave it off. She knows that I know the answer already, and I would only be posing it to make myself feel good. Fishing for compliments.

I don't need them. The compliments. I have a fair amount of confidence that things went well. My mom feels much the same way, that despite my whining about there not being enough cookies around when I was young (there never are enough cookies. How can there be?) that I had a healthy childhood, and by and large a happy time.

What my eldest child sees, is how many people at or around her age are already tarnished, scraped, scarred and troubled by the things they have been told by the people in their life. Unhappiness is more than the weight of all of the things we hear in the news, are fed in our streams. We also pass on bad/sad/mad information out of the blue sky. Maybe some of that information is useful. Some is not so useful. Not necessarily lies, but grim, unsolicited observations about life that have been handed down to them, because that is something we as a species do. *You're unhappy? Too bad. I'm unhappy too. Why bother to do that, nothing will come of it. I don't like your attitude. This is okay, I guess, but it's up to you. You're just asking to be hurt. Why bother? You don't have a chance in hell of making it doing that.* And this kind of bile creeps into the smallest, most mundane things. *You have the same mousy hair as I do, there's nothing you can do about it. Maybe if you didn't eat so many doughnuts, you wouldn't be out of breath walking up a flight of stairs.*

Because, she says, what happens a lot is that people pass on their negativity like seeds to an heirloom garden. They share, unfiltered. They weren't listened to, so they don't listen. They were saturated with criticism in their own lives – in the form of supposedly well-intentioned correction and carrot/stick child-rearing mechanisms – and told what they were doing wrong, wearing it wrong, look silly, smell funny, sound stupid, did it poorly, as a matter of course – so they continue that blockchain with their own children. Poison flows along the most worn path.

She tells me she knows life is going to be hard. Complicated. Full of w*ork*. And her mom and I have prepared her for this. And don't get me wrong – she grouses about the future, like we all do. But she thanks us for not making her feel that work and complication and difficulty are misery. More like…challenge. Find a way to get things done and still be happy. Or at least satisfied that you accomplished something.

I cannot admit to having any credentials whatsoever for getting it right. Rather, I seem to have stumbled into a happy childhood and satisfying youth for my own kids. How did this happen? My own childhood was good, fraught with hurdles I stumbled over, but mostly…fun. And societal circumstances (and my own folks) were indeed forgiving. But for reasons I can only just now see, because they are clearest upon reflection, my parents did not choose to mess me up (in the parlance of that time.) And coincidentally, my girls are happy and healthy.

I am different from you, she tells me. And the same.

I could fill pages with anecdotal evidence of her point: my daughters were, are, good students – different. Curious about art, literature, music, nature and philosophy – same. Stubborn –

same. Attentive – different. Hospitable and welcoming – same. Not easy to give in to anger and frustration – different. Surely some of these traits are part of the package deal of my wife and I – we, too are similar and different. But because I was the home caregiver, I was the parent my girls saw more, heard more from, learned actively and passively from.

I enjoy seeing the results of their growing up. I appreciate our differences. They teach me a lot of things. And they are artists, gardeners, philosophers, readers. Like to cook. Try new recipes. Read recreationally. I love this, because I have heard a statistic that most people never read a book again after they get out of school. And what is up with that?

We Got A Thing And It's Called… – July 2023

It turns out that sometimes the words just don't want to reveal themselves. Does this happen to you? I stumble over a paragraph for a whole day, typing and backspacing in a way that must sound like I'm particularly productive, but which is quite the opposite. I save and save again (I do this manually, even though I know I can set it to do so automatically) but nothing new is added, or even taken away from my WIP.

And I swear I know that I ought to move on, to another paragraph, another thought, another piece of work completely. Start something new, something green and untrammeled by considerations and time. But maybe like you, I'm stubborn, sometimes, in a particular and peculiar way. Like if someone was giving me advice – solicited or otherwise – they might suggest all of those possible solutions and scold me for acknowledging them but not acting. And perhaps they could even offer that a recalcitrant piece of prose sometimes needs to be jettisoned and approached anew on a different day. A Thursday. In August. Don't even save the mess, just open a new file altogether. But no. Those who teach how to overcome errors, sometimes also make them. Or something like that. Just keep typing.

Maybe it's me. Maybe the well is nearing that place where you can't dip fresh water from the top anymore. Or there are so many stories and poems and memoirs being written simultaneously throughout the world that the muses cannot keep up with them all and have some of us on hold. Please stand by. Your yarn is important to us. We will get to you in the order in which you began your tale.

So this spring and summer I open files, gaze at the contents, longingly, lovingly, and fiddle with a word here or there. Save the file with a new name and a new date – more current by weeks and months and feel pretty good about myself. Savor that fleeting sense of optimism that a breakthrough is forthcoming. If not now, then very soon. But it's not here, that breakthrough. Not by a long shot.

I'm OK with this. Partly because if it was easy, everyone would be doing it. Wait – a lot of us are doing it. Revised: everyone would be doing it without complaining.

I keep typing. I just keep typing.

And I am, admittedly, not caught in the nefarious web of publication. Or, rather, the web of submission for publication. A person can handle only so much at one time. When I figure out this particular logjam, the Gordian knot – or in my case the gordian not! – of this problem, I will think about sending things out again.

I am, of course, all over the map.

I know someone who resolves their writing concerns by erasing. That is, they take pages of text and remove words, until they have a poem, or a new philosophy or an advertising campaign slogan or a declaration of war on word processing. Another creates poems by leaving out objects and subjects and the occasional verb. Like writing Mad Libs, only really, really intellectual ones. Well, nearly so, because without nouns and verbs, it ____ just ____. Nevertheless, that's how they make strides forward, grist for the mill. In a similar way, I have attempted Shakespearean sonnets. It's nearly impossible to write one that works within the structure of rhyme and rhythm, much less one that does that and makes sense, much less one that does that and makes sense and is about a subject worth crafting a poem about. I do it anyway. It's a lot like trying to start a car by putting it in neutral and pushing it over a cliff, then dropping it into drive and giving it the gas. It makes my nose bleed. It melts the tips of my fingers.

But here's the thing. No one else cares. No one sees that - the maroon-crusted tissues and band-aids. No one who is worried about my writing problems cares how I scrub this filthy frying pan, how I dig this drainage ditch, how I pull this painful tooth. Only me. I keep typing.

Eventually is my friend. Our relationship is based on trust, like all relationships. I keep typing and eventually the words will come. I keep thinking of new things? One of them will be a story, a character, a fair rhyme. Something not too bad. Good enough for now. Eventually, I'll finish this, and move on to something else.

Midseason – August 2023

I had a sound plan to write about something else, something more "literary" and as such more pertinent to you folks who are the readers. Maybe I could put this off for a month or two. But baseball isn't a month-or-two thing. It's a now thing. The game is tonight. Or this afternoon. He's twenty-four, and will retire soon, in the grand scheme of things. Right this moment, he's flirting with .400, or on a pace to hit 45 dingers. That will change next week. Or perhaps not. (I am hopeful that Mr. Arraez of Miami's Marlins continues to be as hot at the plate as he is today.)

So, no, this can't wait. It'll be around the All-Star game when you open these pages. The middle of the season. For some teams - mine, maybe – it's already over, time to trade the pieces on the board and see what comes of it next year. I have no long-term emotional tie (yes, it's a kind of baseball infection) so I won't become outraged at any changes. I will be, however, discouraged.

I'll have three more tickets to see the Durham Bulls, in my seat up near the rafters behind the visitors' dugout. It is hot there, even in the late afternoon of a July Thursday. Shady, but stifling. I pay for a bottle of water, and maybe some peanuts. I like to shell peanuts and drop the shells on the ground, to step on, crunch, even though to my senior-citizen self it is messy, avoidable. But what does one do with the shells, otherwise? Put them in my shirt pocket? No. It is appropriate to let them fall, like a child would. And I check the major league scores between innings. What is Shohei doing? How are the Cards and Rays faring?

It has been an odd season for me – because in some ways I have lost my compass. For twenty years, I have followed Albert Pujols, from his sophomore year at first with St. Louis, through his salad days, past the move to Anaheim and his inexorable, inevitable winding down. Last summer was amazing, at the age of forty-two back with the Cardinals, he played with, what did Costner call it? "Fear and arrogance." Fear, maybe, because it was all coming to a close. Arrogance because, well, because he was Albert the *Machine*. And now he's home, doing something else. Maybe fixing a light in his kitchen. Running on a treadmill at the gym. Grilling in the back yard. I like to think that he's doing these everyday tasks, sipping a cup of coffee.

But this summer, I look at all of the teams, watch a lot of games, and I'm following anyone or anywhere. This is odd, and I miss looking at the scores for a particular name and contribution.

When I was twelve, I collected baseball cards. A pack of Topps cost fifteen cents. I made a quarter a week allowance, emptying the trash. (I was an awful employee of my mom – who had to constantly remind me not to pour the trash from little cans into bigger cans, but to just carry the little cans out to the bins, one by one. So inefficient, but it had to be done that way because my dad poured his ashtrays into the little cans and if I did the can-transfer, I ended up with ashes all over the carpets. I did it anyway, of course, and sneakered the ashes in so she couldn't see my mess.) Every two weeks I could go with my half-dollar to the luncheonette and buy three "wax-packs" of cards and a nickel-size pack of Bazooka bubble-gum. If I rationed myself, and didn't share with my friends, that would last about a week of hard chewing. I did not put the bubble gum on the bedpost overnight, but I did set it on a square of toilet paper, and then attempted to peel off the bits of paper as best as I could in the morning after breakfast. If I neglected this ritual, my mom always threw it out when she found it later, in what I am certain was legitimate disgust.

I loved looking at the cards, pictures on the front, statistics on the back. It is a funny thing, probably rare now, discovering baseball and baseball cards at around the same time. If you are of a certain age, and a little bit lucky, the cards you get are the players you attach to, a bit like baby ducks bonding with whatever they see first, right after they hatch. Or, maybe that's a…suburban legend, I don't know. Anyhow, my guys were Jim Wynn (the Toy Cannon) and Vida Blue, Cleon Jones and Donn Clendenon and I don't expect any of those names to mean anything to you. And it was a time when parents sometimes got both the morning and the afternoon daily paper, I learned to follow the scores of your team and my teams were the teams of my baseball card heroes. Nowhere at all local to New Jersey, but rather spread throughout the land – Houston and Oakland and Pittsburgh and St. Louis. I thought about those places and the other fans of those teams and our bond with the players. Our common desire for their success, player and team. And then, if someone was traded, saying farewell to that city to follow them to the next landing place – Chicago, Los Angeles, Philadelphia. Their skill, longevity, the color of their skin, didn't matter to me. Only that I had their card.

It's good, I think, to have connections – however tenuous as the whims of a team's general manager – with other places. To feel like the Dominican Republic and Venezuela and Toronto, Canada and Mizusawa, Iwate, Japan are places where real people are born and live and to have those people be important to you.

And it's OK if you don't know what I'm talking about from a baseball perspective. Translate the idea into whatever medium makes sense in your life: novelists and poets and guitar players and movie actors, what have you. Love them in their words on the page, in their concert performance, in the scene on the screen. That's the best way, I think.

Expectations – September 2023

You know what I've noticed? We expect a lot from our writing. That which was once in our heads, pinballing around to get out, put to paper with precision and emotion and complexity and clarity. Scribbling the best we know how. We expect more from our creation than we do from ourselves.

And, therefore, it isn't easy to be happy with what we've accomplished. There is always some other bridge we have to cross. Some other hurdle. Draft finished? Needs revising. Do it. *Do it.* And having revised as much as you are able or willing, it's time to find someone else to read your work. Someone who you know (hope against hope!) will tell you honestly (really?) what their thoughts are about it. Not just the jots-and-tittles of grammar and punctuation – don't get me wrong, these are imperative – but the blunt truth of plot and narrative and style and so on. Where does it ride off the rails. What still remains in your head, yet needs to be on the page?

Was that asking too much to just want to be happy about it for a minute? Feel the warm green grass beyond the finish line under your bare feet? Looking in the mirror and smiling at what you've accomplished. Something tangible, and real. Not perfect – no. But still… Just to appreciate it.

Apparently, yes. It is too much to be happy. No, I don't know why this is so. There's something a little bit off about being a writer, a poet, a playwright.

We can argue about that last statement until the cows come home, and someday we will, but not right now. I want to talk about the happiness thing.

Anyhow, we shared our thing with someone else. In search of

a particular and peculiar validation we are unable to give ourselves.

And then we submit.

I think I'm not saying anything new here. I'm not offering one idea you haven't already heard from someone else or told yourself. That submission is part of a goal. That acceptance through submission is the endgame. Yes, it is difficult to be self-satisfied. Important to value being in the moment, rather than keeping up the momentum. Only natural to let someone judge your work based on simple merit – something resembling an equation of completeness plus our own effort to do well divided by the right time and place equaling, *what?* And to let this new thing, or even this old thing, be…criticized by someone else, is enormous. Full of trauma, or at least drama. (Are these words etymologically entwined? I wonder.)

There are not very fine lines between "he's a smart fellow" and "hey, smart guy" and, finally, "you're a real smart-ass." Wise man and wiseguy. Knowledgeable and know-it-all. Or is it a slippery slope? No, a slippery slope implies that you are falling, or at least at risk of falling. Some kind of inadvertent action, tumbling out of control from one painful-looking bump to another. The fine line, on the other hand, is just there. Like if you reached out your hand, you could almost touch it, anytime you want. And then you're past it. And there's another, perhaps even finer line there, somewhere. Fine lines are like razors – you can touch them, step on them, wander over them, but should you?

My frequent not-so-very-fine line is that crack in the pavement between *what I said* and *what I meant to say.* (In other words, I apologize a lot.) So, smart guy, what did you mean to say? To not give into the social insistence on immediately revealing everything, how much it means to us, what a sacrifice it was to bring into the world. Just be happy about it. Enjoy just being creative.

I don't know about you, but I don't think that's a lot to ask of ourselves. Readership is an artificially created reef for us to founder on. Which is an odd position for an editor to take, yes?

Age – November 2023

Woke this morning with but one errand to perform – to get my driver's license renewed. (I'll be sixty-six by the time you read this. Had to go to the DMV in person to get the task completed.) Well, OK then. Signed in and waited in my car to be texted, per their instructions. And waited.

Sixty-six is a good number. A very fine old highway song. Ten short of the proper number of trombones. I don't feel sixty-six. I'm not sure what I do feel like, but not sixty-six. There's a lot of silly little boy still left in me. Don't believe me, ask any of my friends. They'll vouch for my immaturity in certain matters. And my sincerity that this is the proper way to behave.

I, on the other hand, see myself for what I am. I want to be able to write, and, therefore, feel an inexorable need to be able to dream, pretend, make-believe, and to do that with any success I must keep my childish, childlike perspective. In order to fly, you have to not grow up, not truly, not completely. And, having written those words, I find that even they don't do the idea justice. Maybe because it's not a matter that needs clarification. I don't know. I also don't care.

So, when I go do something *adulty* (the very typing of which undermines and disarms my whole point), like renewing my driver's license, I go prepared. I won't be annoyed by the wait. Oh, there'll be one, and I have nowhere better to be. But I bring a good book. Will there be extra rewards after I'm done? Maybe. Maple-walnut scones are good, I could look for one of those. And a large latte. Sit outside at a table and read a little bit, watch the world go by. Who's hurt by that?

In the meantime, there are five bays with five other driver-wannabes who are taking their tests, standing smiling for their photos, paying their fees. One of them, right in front of my seat, is an elderly woman. She's chatting with the DMV employee about this and that, making conversation. And I'm listening. Long enough to realize that what sounds at first to be what they used to call addle-pated is in fact just friendly banter. This seems to be her manner, I would guess, just to talk with the folks she crosses paths with on a daily basis. Sure, it's slowing things down a little, but who really cares? Or if they do, well, she's earned the right to chatter with strangers.

Little do I know.

It's time for her eye-test. The long and short of it is that this takes a good twenty-five minutes to get through. She starts without her reading glasses, then stops to find them in her handbag, puts them on, takes them off again because they don't improve the situation. Twice she stops to wipe her eyes with a tissue, either because of discomfort from the test-machine she's leaning her forehead against, or because she's realizing how poorly she's doing just trying to read the top row of letters.

At one point, she asks if what she is seeing is a *V*. Yes, ma'am says the DMV employee, in an act of what I consider unusual kindness. Then the woman is informed that she has failed the exam and won't be getting her renewal. She explains that she has a note from her ophthalmologist stating she can see to drive, and she has both faxed it to this office, as well as "snail-mailed" it.

And this is where I realize that this little old lady has dropped a little clue that she is totally *with it*. She's used a term that is only used by people who do email, or DMs. *Snail-mail* implies a practical knowledge of the other alternatives. Or at least, this is what I – and possibly the DMV employee – conclude. Said employee – again, completely out of character – goes off to find that faxed note. And fifteen minutes later, does. And miraculously passes our heroine with semi-flying colors.

And I know it is difficult to believe, but we're not here to make fun of the little old lady, or the DMV. Because what happens next is...remarkable. Confirming her personal information, she informs the DMV person that her birthday is indeed tomorrow and that she will be 94. Ninety-four years old.

Yes.

And my point here, the singular reason for regaling you with this anecdote, is that this is a woman with optimism. She is getting her license renewed when most of us will be, well, no longer driving at best and doing a dirt-nap at worst. We should all have optimism like that, about getting in shape or learning a new skill, growing a garden or doing rewrites on that novel. And no, I don't care how well she drives. In fact, I have but one regret.

Because at that moment, when this woman was standing to get her new photo for her license, they called my number, down to bay 5. And I went down there and didn't get to see the little old lady amble out the door and get into the car that she'd driven there that morning.

I like to think it was a Ford Mustang Cobra. Something her late husband bought long ago, and she would hate to part with it, because it holds corners like it's on rails.

Coming To Grips - March 2024

I saw them outside the coffee shop as I was pulling in to pick up a mid-morning latte. A handful of busy youngsters, standing in front of a folding-table stacked logically with different colored boxes.

Girl Scout cookies.

I slowed, did the math – recalling exactly how much cash I had in the wallet in my back pocket, while simultaneously eyeing a parking space slightly fuddled by a poorly navigated pickup truck. No problem.

Cookies first, then coffee. Why? I don't eat cookies. I'm not allowed to eat cookies. But there are the uniformed saleswomen, all about second or third grade, smiling at me as I walk up. Would I like to buy some? Absolutely. Thin Mints. Shortbread. I part with the cash, for, as the man said, it is money I have.

My youngest selling cookies: how many years back? More than a few.

I would jumpstart the process, by ordering an absurd number of boxes. There may or may not have been awards for most boxes sold, I don't recall. She would camp on the phone with Grandma and Nana – wheedling a double-handful more boxes ordered. Sometimes they wouldn't even get the goods delivered, being out of state. So goes capitalism. Around the neighborhood, I waited patiently (or was it menacingly?) on the street while she rang doorbells, order sheet in hand. Looking wistful, like a Dickens character. *Please, sir, or madam, can you please buy a couple more?*

She faithfully made sales. Less enthusiastically delivered the boxes, when they arrived, filling the back of our minivan. Perhaps that is what makes me think that there was a sales-perquisite she had already received. A stuffed animal of some ilk? A badge for her sash?

So wife and I did the order fulfillment, collections, modifications. Everyone wanted one or two more boxes than they originally thought they did. Late January is a miserable time for most of us. Cookies make it better. So we borrowed some from Grandma and Nana. So it goes. We contacted the scout leader – do you have spare Thin Mints? No? Why not? They're already all gone? What were you thinking when you didn't order an additional 144 boxes, just to be on the safe side? What do you mean, you got stuck with them last year? Why didn't you call me – I would have bought them all.

Sometimes July is a miserable time for some of us. Cookies stored in the freezer until summertime make it better.

It is no surprise that I miss the days when we would all sit on the floor with an open box of peanut-butter cookies and little glasses of cold milk (for dunking, not drinking) and watch *Kipper* or *Caillou* – I can't believe I can remember the names of those shows – and talk about what happened at pre-school this morning. How much she likes painting (like her older sister.) Can we go to the school playground tomorrow and swing on the swings? Yes. Is it OK to play *Zoo Tycoon* later? A very good idea. Finish that cookie and I'll boot it up.

Time, as the ubiquitous they say, marches on. It soldiers forward, or is it scouts? My youngest is now in the spring of her senior year at university. She is tackling courses with names like Coastal Environments, Invertebrate Biology and Animal Phylogeny. Have I mentioned that she knocked Physics II out of the park, much like Shohei walloping an inside fastball? Soon, she may travel to work a distant somewhere other than here. A lump catches in my throat whenever I think about it, while walking around the block, or sitting on the comfy chair in my office, sipping the last bit of cold coffee from a cup she gave me a couple Christmas's past. I want to be a good father, release her into the wild to do what she's ready to do. I also want to be what I think is a protective parent, holding her close. Sometimes they don't seem to mix well. Stay here, I think. Do something where you and I can get lunch together.

Get a grip, the other part of me says, calmly, cool under pressure. I'm trying, I tell the other part. It's difficult. The other part explains - she has places to go, people to see. Animals to feed and care for. More school, maybe. The world is waiting for her.

It's always about the language – April 2024

On a recent visit to the coffee shop, my wife described something – I don't even recall what - to me, saying "…it runs the full gamut…" As a dues paying member of the grammar school police athletic league, I corrected her – the gamut *is* the full – the complete - something. She is quite used to this by now, having me say things that only show that I'm paying attention in a vaguely insulting way – and didn't throw her whole milk latte at me, perhaps because it was an excellent latte, and not worth wasting on me. Literally, (as the ubiquitous they too frequently say.) Told me I was wrong, and gave me a patent-pending shut-up look.

I did shut up. And, because that's the kind of hair-pin I am, when I got home I looked up the definition of gamut (don't judge me).

And found it described as being the complete range or scope of something, as in – and this was their example – *"the* whole *gamut of human emotion."*

Hold on a minute there, pard. If gamut means complete, then why say the "whole complete?" Or, rather, what I should be saying is this is wrong. Bad grammar, right?

But I've always heard the phrase as "running the full/whole gamut." Can it be bad grammar if it's what we've always said? Is there a…a statute of limitations…on mistakes in jargon or idiomatic phrases that eventually permits them to be led over to the light side of the Force?

Of course there is. The Milton I read at gunpoint forty years ago is full of antiquated English (even for forty years ago) and annoying syntactical constructions that we don't use anymore.

Thank God for that. Time's inexorable passage, and the Atlantic Ocean, often divide our language between and betwixt.

So what are the rules? How long do we have to muddle through before we can pitch certain turns of phrase into the trash bin of time? Is it a Somerset Maugham sort of thing, that there's a rule, but no one knows what it is? And are we spending too much precious time thinking about it?

I saw a social media post in which someone asked if readers prefer good grammar in a workmanlike story to spelling/punctuation hiccups in an excellent yarn. Not that they worded their question in this fashion, but this was the general gist of their post. (Which, of course, is one of those pizza pie tautological idioms in that "gist" already means "central idea" which implies generality, anyhow. For crying out loud. It's a wonder we get anything across to one another at all.)

Anyway, I vacillated between wanting good grammar – that is, well edited prose – and a rattling good story.

Why? Well, because I think, (therefore, I deserve heaps of righteous emotional scorn) we ought to rely on good copyeditors to fix faulty grammar and punctuation, or, as an excellent friend calls it, the myriad jots and tittles in a story's layout. But… who's going to make a story a better story? Another writer? Maybe, but probably not. There are definitely rules for that, in the section referencing copyright.

We could fill a book, and mightily boring it would be, with social media's coffee-table discussion about grammar and language and idiom, and the mistakes we keep making, as speaking and writing humans. And most of that would be plagiarism of a sort; tidbits we've picked up from hyped-up memes and other folks' stale jokes. Autocorrect. Possession v plural. Word choice boners. Typographical miscues.

We're beating a dead horse. Belaboring the obvious. Other stale chestnuts.

At least, I think so. Perhaps others consider this a conversational tool, a way to find common ground, by agreeing to others' faults. Perhaps not.

What happens when we read? What is the deal between us? I imagine we enter the compact of author/reader under the assumption that we are equals – two people attempting to make something of the words on the page? Or is the author a higher authority? No pun intended.

Furthermore, what is the relationship between author and editor? Is there a secret handshake there as well? Creator and pre-critic, scribbler and proofreader. Submitter and decision-maker. Shots are fired across the bows. Second spaces after periods, to em-dash or not to em-dash, how many dots in an ellipse, and what the hell is the point of a prologue, anyway? These minutiae of language litter certain online battlefields where word people go to find someone who understands, they hope, their Eliotesque wasteland angst.

As for me, I'm on the fence. I like diving into a story as much as anyone, but hiccup when there are no quotes around dialogue. On another hand, I could care less about one or two spaces after a period. I mean that. I can always care less about something.

Epilogue: The world keeps turning and anyone looking at the writing community's posts would think we've all lost our ever-loving, blue-eyed minds. Something I found in my own notes - *"I made my wife dinner for Valentine's Day* smacks troublingly of cannibalism."

And speaking of the changing language, I recently told my oldest daughter that there was a time when television ads used to try and get housewives to buy a particular brand of dishwashing liquid because it would keep its bubbles longer, and therefore wash more dishes. The selling point was that you saved some number of pennies per meal, and sure, wasn't that what you wanted to do to help out around the household?

Her response to me? Dad, what the fuck is a housewife?

Boom, baby.

171,000 words and not a drop to drink – May 2024

I've been thinking about how it's very strange out there. You know what I mean, and I don't see the need to use a different word, something more specific, more revealing, than "strange" because you do know what I mean. I could, but I won't. English is a big language. Lots of word choices. Some nitwit says there's about a million words in it, but surely some of those are archaic, and some are slang, and many, many are technical terms (and probably a whole hell of a lot are names for medicines which are created on some app designed for such a thing, and run up a flagpole by marketing types that don't give any consideration to the idea that for most of us the name of one blood thinner brand sounds perniciously like institutionalized violence, particularly without the luxury of a pronunciation guideline.) Yet, sometimes we have to use communications shorthand, so that we can more expediently move on and get to the crux of the matter. Or not, because all you asked me was "how you doin'?" and don't really want to know what's actually on my mind, or what my matter-crux is. (There sure is a cultural attention-span deficit isn't th…..?)

I appreciate talking (and writing) and sometimes just bring up topics and dive into them with people I know and those I just meet and sometimes with the butcher or the baker or the baristas at my coffee shop, and then tip them generously because they don't tell me to pound salt or please shut up. It's one of life's daily little miracles, frankly, that they don't.

I suppose the shorthand is helpful. I can say "it's such a weird time to be here," and that sets the table for just about any subject. I do this all the time (not really, a mindless bit of hyperbolic fluff) with my girls, and they nod and we move on. They do the same with me. So let us try it here, while at the same time attempting to tell you something I've been thinking. Let us see if we can't clearly communicate.

I feel bad about it. It (italics mine, and probably difficult to see) being a lot of things – the world, how we live in it, how we aren't able to get along. Bad. Generally speaking, that is. Bad being another of those nearly useless words (and the term "generally speaking" being even more useless. Or less useful. You decide.). I mean, I'm not in pain, except in that way that someone else's pain is sometimes felt by you, inside you, because you want to understand and help share the burden that is pain. Which still isn't clear enough, because what do I mean by pain? Physical? Emotional? Existential?

 Maybe.

It is strange. We should feel bad. Share pain. Not ignore it. And how insufficient are our words? (A rhetorical question, this last.) The ones we most often use, I mean. How vague (and troublingly so) they are when we wield them, like blunt swords on a cluttered, noisy battlefield. We mean well (so we say) and have good intentions (I'm just saying this to get to a point completely my own, but it may or may not be so) and still our language (that is, our use of it) falters, stumbles, falls short. We've embraced (OK, maybe just air-kiss) a culture that rewards brevity, micro-ness, speed, multi-tasking, the tiny, all things flash. Ambiguity. (And yet we don't like editing, self- or otherwise. Go figure.)

But I guess I've belabored this obviousity (obvious and monstrosity, an atrocious amalgam of my own design) - quite enough. Moving on. Let's agree to agree. It's strange out there. Strange times. You feel bad, so I should feel bad. There is pain. In carload lots. It is real. There are things to be concerned about, have puzzlement towards, frustration and anger is real.

Here's the kicker (a term I haven't done the etymology on and can only guess through common use what I mean) – and stay with me on this, because I think it's a doozy: The oddity of life nowadays (for me) is in seeing how little it (that it we referred to earlier) all applies (to me.) Which sounds selfish and confusing, and unremarkable nonetheless. Who among us will deny that they aren't a bit relieved that they haven't had the misery of something going on out there happening to them? And that seems to be where I've landed of late, in that the things that go wrong on a daily basis for most people don't seem to be going wrong for me. Oh, I see the price of food and gas. I see the parsimony of those who have much. Violence. The lying and cheating. The ignoring of the lying and the cheating. And all the confusion.

I see the news, but it only touches me tertiarily (wrong word, but we'll put it in as a placeholder.) Why is that? Why am I so – what is the word? – solipsistic…? My empathy is on the fritz. I want to distribute my feelings freely, but I am having problems doing so. Has this happened before to any of you? A moment where you feel that, rather than being helpful, interested, touched by a situation, you can't get engaged? Where you're not turning your back, but, facing it (again that ubiquitous term) you don't or can't let it in to be processed by your brain and heart?

It is strange that I seem to be able to muddle through. Strange that I seem to be able to muddle through, unscathed. Why is that? Why am I so little affected? Why isn't it the ubiquitous bad (useless generality) for me? It's almost as if I weren't paying attention, distant, entitled. I think I am, but to what end? Maybe I'm not. I want to talk about it, but to whom? Using what shorthand? I don't know.

In any case, as a human being, should I embrace the onset of some kind of inclusion in the suffering? Take my licks? Have a fair (that tabulation on the great ledger of life) amount of that which is coming to me? Stop being so…what? There are so many words that could fill in that blank. Let's go with lucky. And what is luck? Can we define luck without just pasting synonyms onto it? In any case, I don't ascribe to luck. (I could say I don't believe in luck, but luck isn't a belief system, is it? and you might just as easily say it doesn't matter whether or not I ascribe to it, it is.) And, according to the irrational rules (judgment mine - you can't be this, you can't do that. Knock wood, turn around and spit) of luck, in the very act of talking about it, writing it down, I am jinxing myself. Again, something I don't adhere to – the idea that with every consideration there is the risk of causality, however, there you are.

Ah, me. At some point, I'm going to give this all (life, heartache, the universe) more thought. In the meantime, I will go for a walk, eat a plum, smell a rose, sense my guilt.

We Get By With a Little Help… – June 2024

Sometimes, not always, it is satisfactory to just muddle through. To want more – to ask for it – is both fruitless and unnecessary. What we have is enough. Or there is no more to be had. Or there is more, but not for us, and this is understood and if we're not happy or comfortable with that, at least we get it.

At least, I find this to be so.

And just muddling through, when it comes right down to it, is fun, in a solipsistic, perverse rather dense way. On your own, a lone wolf in a big world, there is no one else to thank, blame, ask permission of, apologize to, reflect with, and be angry at when you don't want to look in the mirror. That works sometimes. Not well, of course, but think of all the rewards I just mentioned.

Despite my snarky logic, many is the time when we try to hold the wood still while also wielding the saw. And any success we have with accomplishing a two-person feat alone we attribute to our superior intellect, rather than blind luck. We muddle through and are amazed with how successful we are at the great life game of solitaire. How magnificent! Did you see that we didn't even cheat once? Did you?

We go muddling on, believing a correlation between any previous apparent self-sufficiency and each situation that comes up as we go forward. I did it before, I can do it again. I work best alone.

But, and of course there is always a "but," occasionally more is required. And by this, I mean more, even though you can ask for it and not get it, because there is no more to be had – yes there is, but not for you. *You have enough - t*he ubiquitous voice of authority has spoken.

Still, something else, something additional is needed. Not a magical X factor. Just a little something. An extra hand to hold the wood. A bit of knowledge you don't have time or inclination to acquire. So how to get it?

I'm no expert. Not in anything. Maybe I know a little bit more about…say, the history of the fall of Rome than the person sitting next to you, unless that person is Mary Beard, Oxford Don and professor of classics. (If it is, though, tell her that I'm now exploring her recent volume about the emperors. Excellent read, by the way.) But of how much use is something like that? Not even in polite conversations. So I rely on the brilliance of others to help light my way. And by rely, I mean very little in my life works without my friends.

My friends put up with a lot, being my friends. I'm annoying, in all the ways that word can be defined. I ask for favors. I request assistance. I call them on the phone and regale them with arduous diatribes about etymology, or arcane history, or some obscure technical problem I'm experiencing.

And for reasons I am unable to fathom, they help me. They come over and fix the sticky front doorjamb. They get past my problems with instructions and assemble a bookcase. Come over with a pick-up truck to help clear yard waste I've stored out in the garage, or weed through too much storage on my hard drive.

Do they laugh at my jokes? No. That would be asking too much. Do they correct my grammar? Thank goodness, yes, because it is often flawed.

What do my friends get in return? Well, it feels like not enough. Like I said, I'm not very good at much. Truth be told, I have little that I can offer in return. I can make a pretty good cup of coffee and there's a comfortable seat on the front porch. I listen. I smile. I say please and thank you. I'm there.

Panegyric…Paregoric – July-August 2024

Our language is a real sonofabitch sometimes. It doesn't always play well with others. It argues that you can do just fine with a workmanlike grasp and a little attitude and then smothers you in misunderstanding and incorrect definition, nuance and new usage. And context. And volume. Anger, frustration and distrust.

Lately, I've been talking a lot with my daughters. They are both out of school now, grown up, busy. and full of new knowledge that I want to know, too. (Try saying that five times, fast…) I call them and ask a lot of questions. Dumb ones, too, I'm sure. Things I'm not up-to-speed about. How to get followers on social media. How to do a clip mask in Photoshop. What does this acronym mean, and when do I use it? (Oh, never?)

If I was my younger self, I would be troubled by this role-reversal, but I pretty much saw it coming. There was a time not so long ago when I pedaled faster, in an effort to keep up with the current. Lately, however, I'm reading old books I should already have read, and my music playlist is antiquated. Yes, those are both true and metaphors, simultaneously. The girls understand, and don't seem to mind. They haven't yet put me out to pasture.

In fact, the best part is that they still call. I'm not quite unnecessary but can be a quick reference for certain things (when to use sundried tomatoes), or someone they know they can unload on with no repercussions, particularly with regard to recent events. In the latter, however, despite promising to always answer honestly, I try to avoid the questions I personally don't enjoy answering. Those things I call "Why?" questions. Because *why* is frequently, not always, an opinion. I want to stay in my wheelhouse but *why* makes that difficult.

But one cannot always avoid trouble. I rely on my language skills. My vocabulary, if you will. I may say to them, "I think the question may be the wrong question. Do you mean…." Or, perhaps, "Ask me that a different way. I want to know exactly what you're implying." And we go on. Sometimes we don't get to the point. Sometimes I apologize. (Sometimes this is later.)

I don't do this sort of arguing thing with many people. Why? (see what I mean?) Because I'm not inclined to do so. I could explain why (aargh!) I'm not, but I won't.

Am I getting lazy? Possibly. (probably!) Also, I just don't know why so, so many things happen or are said or thought. I'm not that clever. I always assume the best answer to such questions is "just because…." Or "I dunno…" Rather like I'm either a tired parent or a teenaged boy living in the 1970s.

Both of which I claim some experience in having been.

Personally, I think we're all lazy. Not necessarily with intent, but lazy nonetheless. There was a great interest a few years back in a form of what I call human cataloging, in which persons responded to a series of questions and after their answers were analyzed, were assigned four emotional and intellectual quadrants of traits that were theirs, based on that analysis. They were told by licensed leaders and educators that they had qualities that matched with others, that blended well or possibly conflicted with. The whole process, rather than being even remotely scientific or credentialed, turned out to be something designed as a parlor game by a couple of women back in the 1930s. Still, corporate organizations took it very seriously for a while, and it was at least fun. Fun to take a look at yourself through a new lens. Fun to belong to something as simple as a personality fraternity. Fun like…Astrology?

And, in the end, this team-building exercise went the way of the dodo. But there was one piece of information that stuck with me anyway. The leader always concluded the personality analysis with the comment that our quadrants are not who we are, but the rut that we tend towards. In short, we are often lazy not just because it's easier, but because it is difficult to overcome the inertia, to pull out of a tailspin, to steer a less travelled path.

And I don't want to cast aspersions, but there's been a lot of this going around for a while. Instead of legitimate debate, chanting in a crowd something short and easy, something that rhymes. That's not poetry. Listening to the so-called talking-heads feed us a line and nodding our heads. It's not expertise, credentialed and fact-checked. And so it is with conversation. We have our vocabulary and imagine it does us well enough. Until it doesn't. Until the anger and frustration kick in. *Pick a side. Shut up. Bullshit.* Digging the ruts ever deeper. Imagining we did all we can do? What alternatives are there - everything is shrinking (down to seconds and characters and pixels, etc.) and the quality of human interaction is deteriorating to a point of no return.

I much prefer having the conversation, the argument, where we take the time necessary to parse the situation and find a way to make our considerations heard. *This is good, and that is bad. How do I know? Because I read it in this book or that paper or watched video in which so-and-so stated it. What do you think, and why?* I fear that this last-best ship may already have sailed.

Public Service Announcement – September 2024

I've recently seen a social media post declaring, in large sans-serif letters, that there are story beginnings that publishers won't even read beyond anymore. They, the great and powerful ubiquitous they, will put the *kybosh* on the work if they see that you've begun your yarn with a wake-up call, or a dream, or a character sleeping.

It would seem they've had enough of that so-called trope. And they're bored.

But they – the same ubiquitous ones? I don't know…, also aren't fond of too much talk, either from the narrator or the people in the story. They think character development is tedious. And please stop giving long-winded and colorful descriptions of places, people, things. It's all just too much. They don't care what everything looks like, sounds, smells or feels like. Please get to the point. Tell us what's happening. And if nothing is happening, jump to a place in the story where something is.

What they think we want is to be slapped in the face immediately and often and then quickly told who slapped us, and then what happened to them for slapping us, how we dealt with the slapping and then the end. Like in movies. No, like on Instagram. Having the wife clobber the husband in the face with a pie accidentally frozen so it breaks his nose and everyone laughs and only then do we hope he's taken to the ER. Maybe not, though, because to not take him to the ER, but hit him with a different pie, also frozen, is still kind of funny in a sick way that we all accept now as just fine from sheer frequency and that explanation is not so important or interesting, and so we don't show it (or even tell it) in our narrative.

So what is wrong? Maybe nothing. Maybe everything in the world that storytelling is. I expect readers to have varying tastes, driven by the noise in their lives. I expect writers to try to cater to those tastes, struggling to find the sweet spot, the Goldilocks-zone of writing. But I didn't think that editors have become so…well, not lazy but one-sidedly powerful (and lazy) as to deign to tell the writers what they don't want to see any more of.

It just seems to be reductive reasoning – negation preventing something from ever happening again. And while we're at it, no long sentences. No paragraphs filled with content that lays the foundation and framework through and around which a story can be painted. No more sentences like that last one of mine.

Side question: If we turn writing advice into an algorithm, won't we stop ever getting that thing we at the moment don't want? Like saying I've had pizza too many times this month, and never want to eat it again. Complete madness, right? Of course I want pizza again. Just not this week. Or maybe not until Saturday. Or Friday…

Perhaps we should stop giving each other such…specific and bitter writing advice. Be helpful in our writing groups, without telling each other what we should not do. Don't like terse Hemingwayesque prose? Fine. Don't find Faulknerian verbal gymnastics your cup of sweet-tea? Also fine. I'm not a fan of every style and flavor, either. But saying "don't do this anymore," is feeding the algorithm of limitation. Defending that with "everyone does it, so nobody should do it anymore" is illogical. I am a big fan of variations, of choices, of details, of all shapes and sizes of stories.

You want to tell a story about wizards? Werewolves? Waking up in the middle of a nineteenth-century whale-hunt? Go for it.

Do it with panache and abandon. If you ask for advice, you can listen to it, but you don't have to follow it. Despite what anyone (including your professor or editor or best-friend) says, there are no sins in writing. (Glitches, mistakes and hiccups? Yes. All fixable problems.)

That's it. That's my rant. Take it for what it's worth. And "write what you know?" I'm not happy with that one, either. I know so very little that it's a slap in the face with a frozen crème pie. Write what you feel like writing.

Once more, on writing and rejection… October 2024

I'm having fun at the moment. Every day I sit at the keyboard, and more of my story falls out of my head. It's not all gold, but when it's time, it'll still polish up nicely. And so it's fun. My main character is still a bit of a mystery to me, as they should be. I keep asking them questions, and they tell me the truth about themselves, and I really appreciate that. My MC and I don't pull any punches, and there's been some blood spilled, and we've all learned something. Quantitatively, I'm a good quarter into the WIP, and it's a good feeling to know that there's a lot to go. I reckon it will take me into the new year before I have a good bead on the finish line. I prefer writing when the weather turns cool, looking out the window where I type and seeing the oak tree across the street shed her gown of leaves. My apology, that sounded dirtier than I intended. Ah, well.

I understand not every writer has fun writing, and I'm sorry that this is not the case. I have suggestions, but I'll keep them to myself, as not everyone wants unsolicited advice. In our current environment, unsolicited advice is sometimes triggering, sometimes just annoying. A kind of privilege issue, perhaps. Perhaps not.

So how can I be having fun writing despite recently being rejected – or rather having received a rejection – for a story that had been submitted nearly a year ago. Can't remember sending it, nor the nature of the organization to whom it was sent. Actually, until I received their note, I forgot it was out there. Apparently, we disagree about some things. Okay then. The note I received from them was polite, vague, somewhat dismissive. What else could it be? Nothing about a rejection makes you feel better, not even a good explanation, or advice. See? If unsolicited advice is not good, solicited advice is only slightly better. In my opinion, keep it short and unsweet. *Not going to use your work, thanks. Nothing personal, but not this time.*

And I'm still learning not to take it personally. When I receive a rejection, I treat myself to a nice cup of coffee, or a popsicle or something. Why not? I deserve it. I went through the process, came out on the other side. Rejection is not failure. Not because I learn something from each rejection because that isn't true. I often don't learn anything at all. I did what I could, wrote the story, proofread it, shared it with a couple of people, friends, family. Didn't take the applause too seriously, didn't ignore the critiques. (Didn't necessarily follow the suggestions, either.)

Here's a question: do you care what other people think about your writing? If yes, why? That is, if you think your work is good, then why? Do you write to become read? To what end? Wealth, notoriety, whatever power being a writer of note brings? To prove to someone that your efforts are valid? OK, that's more than a handful of questions. I've been asked the question "why do you write?" myself, and it's a difficult one. Not really, because the answer is "I feel like it, and there's a story I want to tell," but that sounds childish and unintentionally playful, despite how seriously I consider my words. And, therefore, it is difficult to find a way of communicating the "why" factor in my writing. I suppose "why" questions are always the most difficult. They infiltrate so many aspects of life and insist that we qualify what we do or say or think.

Like why am I having fun? You could, if you wanted to, watch me write and find out. Sit at the chair next to mine and observe me typing, stopping, thinking, taking a sip of coffee, saving my file, getting up and walking around a bit, typing another two sentences, leaning back and reading what I've written so far, thinking about a particular word, flipping over to a game of solitaire, coming back when the right word enters my cerebral cortex. Topping up my coffee. Saving my file again. I don't know what you would learn. Maybe the secret. Maybe nothing.

In the end, neither you nor I are responsible to explain our feelings. Not to anyone. And thank goodness for that. Because *I felt like it* is a good-enough answer for a whole lot of inquiries. Why do you write when so much of what you submit to be published is rejected? I felt like it. Why do you write if it isn't fun? I felt like it.

And if that doesn't work "fuck off" is also a satisfying response.

Surreptitiously – Serendipitously – December 2024

I have a lot of things on my mind. I'll bet dollars to donuts you do, too. I suspect it's because there's a lot of noise out there, and the filters in our skulls are having a difficult time determining what is important and what's not – what's truth and what is pure silliness. It's difficult because one person's silliness may just be another's lifeline to the universe. The fateful message in a bottle. In some limited number of characters, or a ten second video. Because we've compressed our communication into small bites. Nibbles, even.

How can we be expected to communicate well with each other with a language like ours, where words mean different things to different folks? We probably agree more than we think we do, but have no way of expressing it.

Although there is a sort of diaspora going on in the heady ether of social media, I still see postings about all sorts of writing-related subjects. Unfortunate decisions to disband major literary mastheads. (Can't imagine what is going through the slushy noggins of the powers that be at a university when they make such a consideration.) Writers getting discouraged because they've been rejected by…and then they list the blue-chip slush piles they've tossed their manuscripts on. Editors giving submission advice in the form of hard and fast rules and regulations.

Recently came across an idea written on a page of a scribble-book in a coffee shop. One of those things left on a table for people to write in or draw on and then leave it for the next person to find, and then, I suppose at some time the person who left it behind comes back to fetch it and read, keep, archive this little paper time capsule. "Time is all we have, and don't." I looked it up: words of an anonymous writer called Atticus Poetry. I'm probably way behind the curve, but I appreciate the pithiness of the sentiment. I am sometimes over-concerned with the things in my life but am becoming more aware of the value of my time, and the time of others. Trying to not waste so much. I know, I know – good luck with that.

Discouraged. I could be one of those people. I recently sent three poems to a magazine, and was politely told no. I've been told no before, but this time I gave it some real thought. They're good poems, well-crafted if I do say so myself, and competently handled. The right words, if you will. And I thought that each pertained to a subject worthy of crafting a poem to begin with. So what did I do wrong?

Answer: nothing. The receiving editors did not think they were a good fit. It's that simple. Not their size, shape, color, style, fabric, season, what have you. No, Garry. But thank you, anyhow.

Take nothing away from rejection, not a new mood nor advice or a correction in your compass heading. The only thing that has happened is your pride has been affected. You've bumped up against something that hurts for a moment. That will pass.

Somewhere out there is a writer having enormous fun. By enormous fun, I mean being a kid again, on a sunny day in mid-summer, fun. Imagine someone telling you when you were ten years old that there were a dozen donuts in the kitchen that had to be eaten or they would go to waste, and would you please, as a favor, do the honors? That level of joy.

I tell you this, because I see occasionally in that some writers aren't having such a good time. They comment in cover letters or social media that they are discouraged by some hurdle or another – finding time to write, getting in the mood to sit down at their keyboard or with paper and pencil in hand, losing their way in their work-in-progress, stumped by the miseries of rewriting, wanting a good editor to help them, struggling with submissions processes, and engulfed in the general malaise of being rejected again and again.

I acknowledge that these are the troubles that writers must navigate to get their work into the hands of readers. On the other hand, this is what comes with the territory. Is it hard work? Yes. Does it seem like hard work to non-writers? I don't know, but who cares? Convincing non-writers is not the writer's job. Entertaining readers is. And is there anything in the world like writing a good piece, and finding a "home" for it? I don't think so.

That being said, here we go with the unsolicited advice I just said to avoid: don't give up. Get back to work. Write more. One word after another. Write every day. Talk about your writing with others. Read other writers' work. Listen, but remember that opinions vary. Send your stuff out. Sometimes the answer is *yes*.

How We See Ourselves – January 2025

Depends so much on where and when. I am old, but not every day, not all of the time. In truth, I cannot always consider the specifics of being old. Perhaps it is when the cold sneaks under the covers at night – a self-inflicted wound, we leave the ceiling fan on all of the time. Or when I give a thought to the seventeen years I've been doing this very thing, typing the preface to an issue, sipping a cup of coffee as my muse. Seventeen is a goodly number of years. Much has come and gone in the meantime, you can wax nostalgic or make your own little happy list of those things. My point is only that I am glad that I am here, with my coffee at this desk in the old dining room of this house in this neighborhood in this town. I'm not always a fan of certain changes and having a place I can go where I belong, well, works for me. This may be different for you. We are each individual in our likes and dislikes. Don't let anyone tell you otherwise.

I am a loner. Or is it a loaner? I'm here, temporarily. Also, at the moment, by myself. You do the math. Alone, I get to pick the music, the temperature of the room, literally and figuratively. And it works better to be alone when you are writing. You can do weird things, like talking to yourself, repeating the same sentence over and over until you fix it. Humming along with the radio, to clear the noise in your head. Staring out of the window at the folks walking their dogs on the frosted sidewalk. Much may be accomplished by doing this sort of stuff. Maybe I'm not a loner, because while I think I do well by myself, I like knowing that there are others out there. You, and them. It is…stabilizing to be aware of you all.

I am a reader. I have five books open on the ottoman behind my chair. If it were in front of my chair, I might resent that the books are in the way of my feet being put up. Can't have that. Five different volumes, each with its own appeal. I stop writing and move to my other chair, which is draped with a blanket – a throw, I am informed – and lean back and pick up one volume and begin on the page at hand. The middle of something. In media res. It is good, I think, when you get older, to be in the middle of things. Yes, that is a clunky sentence, but I'm going to leave it there, anyway.

I am a writer. I have survived the *write what you know* and the *don't appropriate* eras of modern writing history and am quite comfortable in the current *write what you love* period. Even if it is fleetingly brief, I wish everyone would get here and soon. I think it's pretty great. I enjoy working in a personal genre somewhere between the verse of Robert Frost and the prose of Hunter Thompson. Gonzo with a dash of rhyme, if you will. Maybe it works. I don't ask, at least, not often. I'm not certain it's a matter of opinion. I'm not saying that I'm writing in a vacuum, but that when I work it's a solo flight in a very light aircraft. It must be so, or I will never get from point A to point B. Much buffeting from the headwinds, but worth every strange assembly of words.

I am a partner. My wife likes when I read to her, or at least she says that she does., which is the same thing. I can read anything to her, even my own work. She does like when I'm excited about something I've written. The truth is, however, she doesn't always get what I've written. I'm not her "genre." So it goes, as the great man said. I do not take it personally. I try not to take anything personally, when it comes to writing. I am close to my work, but I am not tied to it, on a train-track with the three-fifteen express barreling down on us. That saves a great deal of grief.

I submit work to potential publishing situations, from time to time. It is emotionally consuming to do so. May I also say that I don't know where 400-word stories came from, but it's an oddly specific number of words. What was wrong with 500? I will say this: it isn't enough to tell me I'm in a forest. I need to know what kind of trees I'm seeing. Am I in Oregon, or the Hurtgenwald? Is it raining? Cold? Did I remember my galoshes? The old ones with the hole in the toe, or my birthday present pair?

How 'bout you? Do you let someone else dictate how you write? Do you respond to prompts, or look for validation on your cellphone's panoply of electronic interaction? Do you worry that you are in a slump, or have lost your muse, or your enthusiasm? Where did you last have it? Look there.

Me? I look in the mirror. I receive, they say, a skewed version of myself from this view. A form of bias influences the truth. What I know, because I am told this, is I need a haircut and a shave. Still, I try to not give too much credence to what I see. Is that lemon or butter yellow? I don't know. My mom in her wisdom chose to teach us the world she lives in, one of limited sight. Don't let first impressions have the whole game. Listen to people, to music, to teachers and nature. What bird is that? Feel. Is it cold outside? Wear a coat. Is it January in New Jersey? Wear a coat, even if it isn't cold at the moment. Playing cards with a guy named Doc? Wear a coat. What I know, objectively, is I'm wearing a thirty-seven-year-old sweater, blue, crew-neck. My smile is real, because I am not smiling at my reflection, but at the idea of having one. It is still fun, even at this late date, even in this train wreck. I am almost ashamed at how much fun it is. Perhaps I have a sort of imposter syndrome, in which I think I am a successful writer. Who cares?

I have no other unsolicited advice. Find a place. Be in the middle of things. Don't take your reflection so seriously. Wear a coat. That's enough for now.

My coffee is not hot anymore, but I don't really care and so take another sip. I could heat it up. but I am lazy in that regard. That much is not news. Everyone that knows me is fully aware. I wish I had an almond croissant, but I don't. We downsized to one car (there's a sentence that is rife with privilege) a couple of years ago, so I can't go get one. No, it is the epitome of *foolish* to DoorDash one.

I know, I know: I really need to get over myself.

Garrison Somers lives with his wife in Chapel Hill, North Carolina. He is the editor of The Blotter Magazine and Corner Bar Magazine. His fiction work includes Livie's Lilies, Fish Bait, The Cucaracha, Tall Mary's Short Story and The Comedy Roast of Carroll O'Connor; Live Tonight at the Friars Club. His first collection of essays is Upwards, Dad Words. If you happened to be looking, that was indeed him at the coffee shop, reading Proust very, very slowly.

www.ingramcontent.com/pod-product-compliance
Lightning Source LLC
Chambersburg PA
CBHW051647040426
42446CB00009B/1019